Beyond Technology's Promise takes a hard look at the home computing scene. How are children using computers at home? Is home computer use related to academic achievement? The research reported in the book focuses on whether families are using computers to help children learn academic skills and, if so, how well they are doing it. Using the acronym SITE (for Studies of Interactive Technology in Education), the three-year, qualitative investigation provided contextual information crucial to our understanding of how computers are really being used. The authors propose directions that must be taken in order to facilitate the educational use of home computers or any other promising educational technology. In so doing, they examine such topics as parental leadership, the home–school computer connection, and the role of gender in home computing use.

Beyond Technology's Promise

Beyond Technology's Promise

An Examination of Children's
Educational Computing at Home

JOSEPH B. GIACQUINTA

JO ANNE BAUER

JANE E. LEVIN

CAMBRIDGE
UNIVERSITY PRESS

Published by the Press Syndicate of the University of Cambridge
The Pitt Building, Trumpington Street, Cambridge CB2 1RP
40 West 20th Street, New York, NY 10011-4211, USA
10 Stamford Road, Oakleigh, Melbourne 3166, Australia

First published 1993

Printed in the United States of America

Library of Congress Cataloging-in-Publication Data
Giacquinta, Joseph B., 1937–
Beyond technology's promise : an examination of children's
educational computing at home / Joseph B. Giacquinta, Jo Anne Bauer,
Jane E. Levin.
p. cm.
Includes bibliographical references (p.   ) and index.
ISBN 0-521-40447-9. – ISBN 0-521-40784-2 (pbk.)
1. Computer-assisted instruction. 2. Children – Education – Data
processing. 3. Home and school. 4. Microcomputers. I. Bauer, Jo
Anne. II. Levin, Jane E. III. Title.
LB1028.5.G45 1993
371.3'34 – dc20   93-204444

A catalog record for this book is available from the British Library.

ISBN 0-521-40447-9 hardback
ISBN 0-521-40784-2 paperback

To

Benjamin Giacquinta, Tom Veltre, and Florence and Bernard Levin,
each of whom in his or her own way made the writing
of this book important.

Contents

Contents

Tables and Figures

ix

Preface

Personal computers have become so widespread in the United States that they are now indispensable to our business world, prominent in virtually all educational settings, and present in many millions of homes. If one looks at the current literature written by the proponents of computing, the educational world looks exciting. Computers will act as catalysts, stimulating teachers to rethink the educational process. Computer integration into the curriculum will mean that children will learn *with* computers, as well as *about* them. Moreover, many educators have progressed from considering computer use as a means of helping children acquire basic skills to connecting the use of computers with exciting and invigorating ideas about how people learn and about school reform. The use of computers is also tied in with many current ideas in education – the importance of intrinsic motivation, learning by doing, cooperative learning, apprenticeship, children as designers, and parental involvement.

Just as there has been great promise for computers in school, so has there been for computers at home. Computers at home, advocates maintain, enable parents to help their children to learn in ways that never before were possible. While a great deal of research has gone into what has happened to computers at school, next to nothing has been devoted to computers at home. Our book attempts to contribute to this vital yet unstudied area. It reports the results of an analysis of qualitative information gathered on seventy families during a three-year period from early 1984 through 1986. It deals with the problem of getting beyond the promise of a technology to a social reality that satisfies the dream.

As we finish the writing of this book in the early 1990s, new computer-related technologies are being promoted as vital adjuncts to the education of children. We believe that these, too, will be subjected to the principles and forces uncovered in our work. The lessons learned from our study are therefore particularly important if other promising technologies, as well as computers, are to have positive effects on children's learning at home and at school.

This book is intended for a wide range of professionals whose interests and efforts are related in one way or another to the use of computers for education: advocates of educational computing, creators and distributors of educational software and hardware, researchers in educational computing, and scholars of educational and technological change at home and at school. While the book was written specifically for such people, we believe many school administrators, teachers, and parents will also find it valuable. Because we wrote it for such a diverse audience, some rather extensive endnotes and several appendixes are included for readers who may not be familiar with one or another topic or who may want more information. For example, for the technologically minded readers who are unfamiliar with organizational change, we present an extended endnote in Chapter 10 about the fundamental questions posed over the years by researchers in the field of planned change. For those unfamiliar with the current concern over home–school relations, the lengthy endnote in Chapter 11 might be useful. For researchers who may have wanted more specifics about our research procedures as discussed in Chapter 2, we present additional materials in several appendixes. When we thought that ideas were important but would interrupt the flow of the chapter, we put them into endnotes.

It would have been impossible to complete the fieldwork, analysis, and writing of this book had it not been for an enormous number of people. First, we wish to acknowledge our indebtedness to the seventy families – the parents and children

– who gave so unselfishly of their time and energy so that we might better understand what was happening in homes with computers and why. It should be noted that all of the families and family members named in the book have been given pseudonyms in order to protect their anonymity. We also want to thank the seventy fieldworkers who spent so much time and effort in homes observing families around their computers as well as asking them questions about their activities and feelings. Indeed, the data gathered were so rich that the task of analysis was made truly formidable.

As with any large-scale research, many people other than the researched and the researchers made this project possible. We want to thank Dick Robinson at Scholastic, Inc., whose interest in what was happening in homes with computers led him to give the School of Education at NYU a grant to pursue this question. Had it not been for his generosity and the support of the then dean Dr. Robert Burnham, his assistant Dr. James Finkelstein, and Associate Dean Dr. Gabriel Carras, this project could never have gotten off the ground.

It is also important to thank Professors Margot Ely and Trika Smith-Burke who in the early years along with the senior author were instrumental in getting the project under way. Marsha Lichtman, the project's first graduate assistant, helped structure what at the beginning was often unfocused. During the middle years of the project, Peggy Ann Lane, as an Assistant Research Associate, gave much of herself in running the everyday operations of the project as well as in reading and editing project reports. Her efforts were pivotal in the project's successful completion. In the later years the three authors were joined by Peggy, Mike Caruso, Ellen Katz, and Inez Wolins in formally analyzing the log materials and written materials generated up to that point. We want to express our deep-felt gratitude to them for their outstanding contribution.

We are grateful to the anonymous reviewers for their reading of our book proposal and its first full draft. Their comments strengthened considerably the book's form, logic, and substance. We also thank Barbara Uhl who, as a teacher, gave us a very careful reading of our first draft. Her many thoughtful comments encouraged us both intellectually and emotionally.

Finally, we wish to thank Julia Hough, our editor at Cambridge University Press. It was she who saw the value of our work and who gave us the leeway and the time to do the book our way. We will always remember her patience and support.

With regard to authorship, it should be noted that the names of Bauer and Levin are listed alphabetically.

J.B.G.
J.A.B.
J.E.L.

Chapter 1

The Promise

It seems that the message the parents are buying, along with their home computers, is pretty clear: one way or another – both in school and at home – computers can help American education pull itself up by its bootstraps. (Komoski, 1984, p. 245)

Home computing became a reality in the late 1970s after Steven Jobs and Stephan Wozniak, working in a garage, created their stand-alone *micro*computer, the Apple.[1] In their book *Silicon Valley Fever*, Rogers and Larsen (1984, p. 11) describe the Apple's inauspicious "birth" and the poor impression it made on computer figures like Nolan Bushnell:

Jobs and Wozniak . . . went to their bosses at Atari and Hewlett-Packard with it. Jobs tried to convince Nolan Bushnell, founder of Atari and creator of Pong, the first video game, that microcomputers had a bright future. But computers were not in Atari's product line, and Bushnell laughed at Jobs.

Nearly ten years later, however, Bushnell ruefully recalled: "We all knew that profits were in mainframes and minicomputers. That was in 1975. . . . I never said we were perfect." By 1982, when *Time* named the personal computer its "Man of the Year," sales of microcomputers had topped $5.4 billion (Rogers and Larsen, 1984, pp. 11–12).

Rogers and Larsen (1984, p. 17) also point out that the promise of the personal computer could not have been fulfilled without the "thousands of software programmers around the country" who had ideas about how the Apple could be used for education and for other purposes:

When the hobbyist market for microcomputers dried up in 1978, dozens of little computer firms collapsed. But not Apple, thanks to its cadre of free-lance programmers who had designed accounting, word processing, spelling, teaching, graphics, and a host of other programs. By 1983 over 15,000 programs were available for the Apple computer.

The development of the personal computer and software, as important as they were, might have had little or no educational impact had it not been for the growing disenchantment with public schools and the publication of several reports in the 1980s critical of public schooling. These included *A Nation at Risk* (1983), *A Nation Prepared: Teachers for the 21st Century* (1986), and *Making the Grade* (1983). Taken together, these reports revealed just how ineffective reformers, educators, and parental groups believed the public schools to be.[2]

THE EDUCATIONAL PROMISE

Many reformers saw the newly created personal computer and the growth of educational software as fundamental to the improvement of public education. With the computer-aided instruction of the 1970s in mind, some software creators, educators, and parents formed alliances to put computers into the schools, thereby hoping to make them more efficient and effective places for children to learn. Equally important, they urged parents to buy computers so that children could use them at home in cooperation with the school.

Other reformers, having given up on school improvement, argued that education could be changed dramatically if computers were brought into the home because they would enable parents to help their children learn in ways *independent* of the schools. Some even said that this move could revolutionize the way education took place in America.

The vast literature on educational computing reflects two somewhat divergent views of its educational promise for families: (1) that children's use of home computers would increase their learning or academic achievement at school, and (2) that home computers would empower parents to educate their children independently of the school.[3]

It was hoped that the computer would be used at home as – in Taylor's (1980) terminology – a tutor, a tool, or a tutee. With the appropriate software, it would tutor children in their learning of subjects (e.g., math and science) and skills (e.g., reading and writing). It would also help children develop thinking or problem-solving skills. As a tool at home, the computer would help children accomplish such tasks and activities as writing and editing, manipulating data, drawing, composing music, and telecommunicating. As a tutee, it could be programmed by children to accomplish various educational tasks.[4]

REASONS FOR THE OPTIMISM

In the past, technologies such as radio and television were expected to transform education, but none has reached its potential as a learning tool (Cuban, 1986).[5] No tool before, however, seemed to hold out the educational promise of the computer. Rogers and Larsen (1984) attribute the hope that was pinned on the computer to its interactive potential: "What is different and special about computers is that they are interactive. It is this interactive nature of computers, and of related communication technologies based on computers, that marks a cultural turning point from the passivity of viewing television" (p. 260).

Wakefield (1983, p. 1), too, was optimistic about the computer's interactivity and its potential for encouraging children to learn at home:

> With its powerful interactive potential, the computer used for education emphasizes learning rather than teaching, the student rather than the teacher. This permits the students to work with a greater degree of independence from the school and teacher, and shifts the locus of learning from the school to the home as more homes than schools get computers.

3

Speculating about how this technology would revolutionize learning, Komoski, quoted in Wakefield (1983, p. 1), went even further:

> It is not being overly pessimistic to view the microcomputer as the vehicle that may drive a technological and instructional wedge between the home and school. . . . On the other hand, it is not overly optimistic to think that educational computing could become the basis for cooperative, community-wide educational experience for all families.

In short, the 1980s saw the spread of a technology that many came to believe had great promise for solving some of American society's urgent educational problems. Not only might computers become integrated into classrooms, but they might also provide parents with a tool that could enhance their children's achievement at school or help them educate their children on their own. The time of the home computer in the field of education *seemingly* had come.[6]

THE MEANING OF
EDUCATIONAL COMPUTING

The term "educational computing" has been used in a variety of ways. Some have maintained that *all* computing is educational in one way or another. For instance, computer games, even those not labeled educational, can help players develop eye–hand coordination, spatial skills, and higher-order thinking skills.

With a more specific definition of educational computing in mind, schools began introducing children to computer literacy and elementary computer programming about a decade ago. They also began using academic drill and practice software with some students.

In this book we use "educational computing" to refer to any educational endeavor in which the computer is used. Such endeavors include fostering computer literacy, programming, word processing, and educational telecommunicating, as well

4

as academic teaching. We use the term "academic computing" to mean the use of computers for developing skills and knowledge and for understanding subjects such as reading, math, science, and social studies.

OUR RESEARCH FOCUS

As we noted earlier, schools have been under attack for some time because they are perceived as being unable to teach basic skills and academics or to motivate children to learn. When personal computers came on the market, they were sold to schools as a promising educational technology for teaching the three R's and other academic subjects and skills efficiently and effectively. Parents were also told that it was essential to have computers in the home if they wanted their children to learn well, achieve better grades in school, and be successful as adults.

Although a great deal of theorizing and research was devoted to school computing in the early 1980s, very little attention was given to home educational computing. Therefore, little was known about the ways in which parents were allowing and urging their children to use computers at home. How was this use being affected, if at all, by their school use, especially with regard to the learning of academic skills and subjects? Were parents helping their children use home computers to improve their performance in school or to learn independently of school? In other words, to what degree were the two versions of the educational promise being fulfilled?

This book attempts to answer these questions.[7] It is the product of a three-year, qualitative field investigation entitled Studies of Interactive Technology in Education (SITE) involving seventy families. The research began in February 1984 and ended in late 1986.

Although we focused on academic forms of educational computing, our qualitative approach allowed us to observe the extent to which children were using their computers for other purposes such as word processing, programming, telecommunicating, and game playing. The study therefore provided contextual information about the presence or absence of recreational and other educational uses of computers at home.

OUR BASIC FINDINGS AND THEIR IMPLICATIONS

Our in-depth study of seventy families revealed a near absence of children's academic computing, only a modest amount of other forms of educational computing (including programming and word processing), and almost no telecommunicating. Game playing took up most of the children's computer efforts in these families.

Children did not use their home computers for academic learning mainly because of social reasons: parents neither encouraged nor aided such computer efforts; schools emphasized other forms of use; and peers and siblings were not supportive of this kind of use. Other social factors that explained why children did not get involved in academic or other kinds of educational computing included parent reluctance – especially of mothers – to use computers; parents' lack of knowledge about or positive evaluation of relevant educational software; and poor communication about educational computing between the home and the school and between the creators of hardware and software and families.

Our research pointed to three overarching lessons about the use of computers at home, lessons that are relevant for other educational technologies as well. Advocates need to (1) more clearly define the social envelope – especially the roles parents and children need to play in order to use computers for academic and other educational purposes at home; (2) pay greater attention to the conditions necessary for the successful diffusion, adoption, and implementation of academic computing and software; and (3) reexamine the adequacy of schools as linking agents to foster educational computing in the home. Unless these lessons are heeded, home academic computing is unlikely to grow very much.

In recent years, researchers and reformers in computers and education have begun to emphasize the potential of computers for learning higher-order thinking skills; for managing and manipulating information; and for creating text, graphics, and music. Many now consider it important for people to use computers as tools, as extensions of the mind, and not solely for the transfer of knowledge. Moreover, computer hardware and software are becoming so sophisticated and powerful that computers are now being hooked up with other technologies to form promising new interactive multimedia for learning. If reformers, developers, educators, and families do not take seriously the lessons learned about simple academic computing at home, however, the interactive multimedia or any other new technology are likely to have little more success in meeting their potential. Here, too, it is necessary to plan for and implement social change. We believe this book has important implications for the effective use of any new educational technology at home or, for that matter, in school.

WHAT THIS BOOK IS NOT ABOUT

There are at least three important issues concerning educational computing in the home and at school that this book can only deal with tangentially at best. One is whether or to what extent computers *should* be used for educational purposes.[8] A second concerns computer equity.[9] The third is related to the effects of computer use on learning.[10]

Whether computers should be used in education remains a controversial question (e.g., compare Weizenbaum, 1976, and Papert, 1980). We recognize how easy it is to misuse or overemphasize computers, but we also believe that with forethought and planning, computers and other technologies can be extremely valuable educational tools.

The point we wish to make is that the use of computers needs to be evaluated with a critical, but not negative, eye. Obviously, technology is here to stay; it has always been a major component of societies, big and small, ancient and modern. All technologies have their "upside" and "downside." What we caution against is the mindless or unexamined use of technology just because it is there. We also warn against the knee-jerk refusal to try a technology just because it is a technology. In short, while we think the contribution of home and school computers to the education of children has not yet been fully demonstrated, we believe that this technology deserves a fair test.

The matter of computer equity with respect to such factors as gender, social class, and race has sociological and political dimensions that go beyond the focus of our research, especially since the data were collected from a relatively homogeneous group of mostly middle-class, white families. We do, nevertheless, speculate about social class differences at several relevant points. We also devote a whole chapter to gender differences surrounding the use of computers.

The proper study of outcomes would have required a different orientation and research design, one that emphasized larger numbers of children and a quantitative approach to data analysis. In addition, had we chosen to do an effects study, we probably would not have been able to get close enough to the families to examine how and why computers were being used educationally at home. Most important, we believe that effects studies are premature when the facts of actual implementation or use have not been established. As Gross, Giacquinta, and Bernstein (1971, p. 216) put it:

> Many promising educational innovations have been rejected on the basis of experimental designs that failed to take into account that the innovations may have been inadequately implemented. Clearly, when a new program or practice has not had a "fair" trial, judgment about its educational utility must be held in abeyance.

AN OVERVIEW OF THE BOOK

In Chapter 2, we provide a brief review of the research conducted on families with computers up to the time of our investigation. We discuss the advantages of doing in-depth

8

qualitative work to understand better the actual educational computing efforts of families. We also describe our research procedures, the kinds of families studied, and the extent to which they represented families with children and home computers throughout the United States – then and now. In Chapter 3, we describe the reality of home computing as we found it, especially the nature of children's academic forms of computing. We also propose a general model for why children do or do not engage in home academic computing. This chapter sets the stage for the next five chapters, which provide further details on the various conditions behind the lack of academic computing at home and discuss possible changes since the end of our study. In Chapter 4, we deal with various aspects of educational software, particularly its availability and quality in SITE homes as well as in the marketplace. In Chapter 5, we discuss the extent to which parents offered encouragement and assistance in order to foster their children's academic and other educational computing efforts. We delve into the reasons why some parents were involved, while most were not. In Chapter 6, we take up the special matter of mothers' reactions to home computers and the reasons why so many feared or avoided them. In Chapter 7, we examine the forms of computing that schools emphasized and the effects of school use on home computing. In Chapter 8, we consider why so many children used their home computers for playing games rather than for educational computing.

Chapters 9 through 11 discuss the three major lessons learned from our study. In Chapter 9, we explore the concept that technological change requires a proper "social envelope" if the technology is to achieve desired outcomes such as the learning of academic subjects. In Chapter 10, we view technological change as a social process depending on a variety of conditions that need to be fostered if a technological change effort is to succeed. In Chapter 11, we discuss the need for an effective linking agent for the diffusion, adoption, and implementation of home educational computing and the role that the school can play in this regard. In Chapter 12, we recap the promise and the reality based on our findings. We discuss one new educational technology – interactive multimedia – and explain why creators and advocates may repeat the mistakes with this and other promising technologies if they fail to heed the lessons learned in our study about academic computing at home. The chapter concludes with suggestions for future research on educational computing.

NOTES

1. In this book, we use the term "computer" to refer to the machine called a "microcomputer" in the late 1970s to middle 1980s: a self-contained machine that (1) is based on the microprocessor, (2) has a video display, (3) can have information read into it by means of disk drives and diskettes, and (4) can be hooked up to a printer and a modem. The term "microcomputer" was used to distinguish this machine from the larger mainframe computer, which dominated business and industry at the time. We shall use "computer," "personal computer," and "home computer" interchangeably to refer to this kind of machine. When we talk about a home computer, we mean it literally: a stand-alone (personal) computer that is located at home. We do not use the term in its earlier sense of a very small stand-alone that was suitable for the home but not work.

2. For a critical appraisal of these and other reports at the time, see Berman's "The Improbability of Meaningful Educational Reform" (1985, pp. 99–112). The disenchantment with public schools did not begin with these reports. It may be that this disenchantment began in the 1960s with the publication of James B. Conant's *The Education of American Teachers* (1963). His critique and those of others such as James Coleman in *Equality of Educational Opportunity* (1966) helped form the basis of the federal government's Great Society initiatives of the 1960s and 1970s, including those for compensatory education. Some critics complain that schools continue to produce a work force that is not skilled enough to support America's large industrial-based and information-based society (Besser, in press). Others have emphasized the seeming failure of public schools to bring about social equity at a faster pace and greater social achievement within its multicultural population. Still others worry about America's flagging efforts to maintain its place

internationally, something exacerbated by Sputnik and the more recent economic competition with other industrialized countries.

3. We chose to study what we believed to be the two fundamental promises of educational home computing. But new technologies can have almost as many "promises" as the mind permits, and those promises can change and multiply as time passes, as illustrated by de Sola Pool's (1983) survey of preliminary assertions and forecasts about the telephone and the telephone system. He unearthed more than 180 such comments in writings from between 1876 and 1940. This number did not include the many assertions that have been associated with its relation to the ongoing computer revolution.

4. Some educators consider simulations a separate category. A simulation program presents a model of an environment (real or imaginary) with which one can interact by exploring or manipulating variables and testing hypotheses.

5. Recently there have been many promising social innovations directed at the organization of schools and classrooms. This list includes such proposed organizational changes as individualized instruction, nongrading, open education, school-based management, school vouchers, and team teaching. The list of proposed technological changes dates back to such entities as chalkboards, textbooks and workbooks, typewriters, filmstrips, radio, movies, and more recently, instructional television, hand calculators, and computer-assisted instruction. Some of these innovations have dealt with the *management* of schools. Others have focused on the *goals* of schools by proposing classroom changes to foster children's academic learning and skills, higher-order thinking, and motivation. For critical views of the probable success of computers in the classroom, see Oettinger (1969), Sloan (1985), and Weizenbaum (1976).

6. For the most recent statement of how home computers might empower families educationally, see Perelman (1992). FOR A GENERAL TREATMENT OF FAMILY EMPOWERMENT IN A RANGE OF AREAS SEE SUSSMAN (1985).

7. In late 1983, Scholastic Inc., an educational publishing corporation that recently entered the home computer magazine and software fields, provided the School of Education at New York University with a substantial grant to study the impact of computers on families. Scholastic was especially interested in promoting research on the educational impact of these machines on

children at home; this topic was a central interest of the principal investigator of the project and senior author of this book. In June 1984, the U.S. Department of Education invited the principal investigator to Washington, D.C., to participate in a conference on the educational impact of home computers and to review early findings of the SITE project. The Department and conference participants were also interested in finding out whether children were using these machines at home for academic subjects and skills and, if not, why not.

8. Although he does not appear to provide a definitive answer, Ragsdale (1988) offers a wide-ranging discussion of the issues related to the "simple" question: Do we want to promote the use of computers in education at school and at home, and, if so, in what ways?

9. For an excellent literature review on computer equity, particularly as it relates to schools, see Sutton (1991). In this extensive article, Sutton focuses on a variety of issues including gender, social class, and racial inequalities in the access to computers. She argues that the use of computers has maintained and exacerbated such inequalities and that equity issues are complex. She recommends that future research explore computer access, processes, and outcomes among poor and minority children and compare the computer endeavors of schools serving more affluent families with those serving less affluent families.

10. By computer effects studies, we mean those that consider whether a certain kind of computing does indeed raise the levels of children's achievement in such areas as math and science or reading and writing. Other "effects" areas pertain to aspirations and attitudes. For reviews of research on the effects of school computing, see Berger (1989), Hess and McGarvey (1987), Perkins (1985), Roblyer, Castine, and King (1988), Schulz (1991), and Sutton (1991). Thus far, these analyses indicate a mixed view of the effects of school computing on children's learning and attitudes.

Chapter 2

Studying the Promise

Qualitative methods can be used to uncover and understand what lies behind any phenomenon about which little is yet known. It can be used to gain novel and fresh starts on things about which quite a bit is already known. Also, qualitative methods can give the intricate details of phenomena that are difficult to convey with quantitative methods. (Strauss and Corbin, 1990, p. 19)

Educational and social science investigations are broadly classified as either qualitative or quantitative in form.[1] In the first part of this chapter, we discuss the decision to study family computing qualitatively. Then, we review some of the study's more salient fieldwork activities and log-analysis procedures. In the final section, we compare the seventy families studied. To simplify the discussion, the words "we" and "our" are used throughout the book, even though Bauer and Levin were not involved in the early SITE decision making and fieldwork.

PRIOR RESEARCH ON EDUCATIONAL HOME COMPUTING

At the time the SITE study was designed, information about children's educational computing at home was largely found in articles in the popular press and in computer magazines.[2] These articles were based on market researchers' quantitative surveys about computer hardware and software and on reporters' qualitative portrayals of families. Both approaches to gaining information about educational computing at home, however, contained serious flaws.

LIMITATIONS OF THE MARKET SURVEYS

The measurement and sampling methods of the early market surveys left their findings suspect. The assessment of *educational* computing in families was usually peripheral to the main purpose(s) of these marketing surveys, and respondents were simply asked to indicate whether their computers were being used for educational purposes or whether they had specific types of educational software. Few, if any, included follow-up questions about the degree of children's home educational computing or about the possible conditions behind different degrees of use. Change over time in educational computing activities or attitudes was also of little concern, and little effort was made to establish the accuracy of family-member responses.

In addition, the sampling tactics used in these studies left the validity and generalizability of their findings open to question. Families were drawn largely from industry-generated sampling frames that were narrow in scope. For example, some consisted of computer-magazine subscriber lists. Other listings came from the mailed-in warrantee cards of particular purchasers of computers, ancillary hardware, or software during a specified period of time. Such lists – limited by topic, geographic area, and time – created considerable potential for sampling bias, even when samples were of adequate size. The way names were drawn from such listings was usually not discussed, although it appeared that either the entire list or some "convenient" portion was surveyed. Finally, when return rates were reported, they were extremely low.

SHORTCOMINGS OF THE EXISTING CASE STUDIES

The case studies of families also had important limitations beyond the difficulty of generalizing from their results. Most were anecdotal descriptions based on short interviews or one home visit by a reporter. The biases of the reporter were never taken into account. Furthermore, few reporters attempted to observe the actual computing efforts of parents and children or to verify the information provided by the families.

As in the case of the market surveys, these portrayals dealt minimally, if at all, with why children were or were not engaged in home educational computing. No follow-up visits or questions were in evidence, and cases were not compared. To stimulate reader interest, authors used exceptional or "newsworthy" families. In sum, the optimistic picture painted of children's actual educational computing at home and the reasons for it were incomplete and inconclusive at the time the SITE study was being designed.

THE QUALITATIVE DESIGN OF THE SITE STUDY

We decided to use a qualitative approach in order to improve upon some of the earlier efforts and to help set the stage for sound future studies of children's home educational computing.[3] We reasoned that it was critical to gain a thorough understanding in selected homes of what was happening and why. Only then would it make sense to employ large-scale quantitative surveys to determine whether the descriptions and explanations uncovered were generally true across the growing number of families with children who owned home computers.

BENEFITS OF QUALITATIVE DESIGN

The qualitative approach provides a strategy for better understanding unstudied or misunderstood social phenomena and their determinants. It also permits the researcher to generate hypotheses and theories about such phenomena. In addition, qualitative designs yield information from a variety of sources, and the findings can be cross-checked so as to ensure a high degree of accuracy and certainty. Qualitative designs lead to an in-depth understanding not only of phenomena but also of processes and their outcomes *over time.* Hence, changes in a situation can be documented and the forces behind such changes uncovered.

Furthermore, qualitative designs make it possible to pursue many avenues of study and to make choices about the importance of emerging factors *during* the investigation. As a result, one is able to alter the research focus so as to include factors that were unanticipated at the outset of fieldwork. The qualitative approach also allows one to test alternative explanations, to resolve seemingly conflicting findings, and to gather new data once gaps in descriptions or explanations are recognized. To put this all in a larger perspective, the strength of the qualitative design is its potential internal validity.

Through qualitative research we could establish whether the market reports and case vignettes were actually overstatements or merely temporary states of family computing. Perhaps families were only rarely or sporadically doing something with their computers. There is no way of judging the accuracy of reported actions without being there to talk to *and* observe families *in situ* over a period of time. If actual observations of behavior corresponded to what members said they were doing, then the validity of verbal reports would be established. If we found conflicts in what they said they were doing or in the reasons why they reported doing them, then we would be in a position to dig more deeply and explain the discrepancy. Clearly, we would be able to provide a more convincing portrayal of what was happening at home than that obtained from reports based on parents or children *telling* researchers or reporters what they were doing with their computers.

MINIMIZING A MAJOR WEAKNESS

If the great strength of qualitative designs is their potential internal validity, the most commonly mentioned shortcoming is the uncertainty of their external validity. Since qualitative field studies most often examine one or just a few instances of a particular phenomenon, there is little certainty that the findings, though accurate for that particular instance (i.e., they have internal validity), are applicable in general (i.e., have external validity). We tried to offset this potential shortcoming by doing in-depth studies of a relatively large number of diverse cases.

Although remaining fundamentally a qualitative study, our study therefore gained an important quantitative dimension as well. We reasoned that if the results uncovered were consistent across a large number of cases studied in depth, we would feel more confident that our findings could be generally applicable. Moreover, if we discovered deviant cases, then their explanation or integration with the more typical cases would further strengthen our understanding of this relatively complex phenomenon.

GENERAL QUESTIONS ASKED OF ALL FAMILIES

Families were told that the general purpose of the research was to understand better how adults and children in families were responding to their home computers. And, although each case was guided by a large number of queries specific to the family under study, the following broad questions were common to all: (1) How and why did the family purchase its computer(s)? (2) What kinds of peripheral hardware did the family own? (3) What kinds of software were present? (4) In what ways were the machine(s) and software being used and by whom? (5) To what extent were children engaged in educational computing and other kinds of computing at home? (6) To what extent were the home computing activities of children influenced by their schools or by other social or personal conditions? (7) What meaning(s) did the computer(s) have for various family members? (8) What impact, if any, did computing have on individual family members and on the family structure? (9) What remained stable in the family and what changed during the research with respect to computing and why?

FIELDWORK ACTIVITIES IN BRIEF

Each of the families was studied by a different fieldworker for roughly four months during the period between February 1984 and January 1987. Fieldworkers maintained regular contact with their families during these four months. There were usually six to ten visits, each lasting one to three hours. These visits were often supplemented by phone talks.

Fieldworkers engaged in a great deal of informal interviewing and observation, and they maintained a running log of their interviews, observations, and reactions – both personal and analytical – to what they were seeing and hearing. They updated their logs after each visit. The fieldworkers' analyses of entries helped shape their next visits and their observations of and interviews with family members. They also wrote periodic analytic memos on emerging computing patterns. (See Appendix A for more discussion of SITE fieldwork procedures.)

ANALYSIS OF FIELDWORK LOGS

The three-year SITE effort produced thousands of pages of log material and analytic papers. In February 1987, as the fieldwork for the last of the case studies was completed, the three present authors and four colleagues developed an initial codebook for carrying out a comprehensive content analysis of all the cases. An earlier analysis of the first eighteen cases had produced a tentative explanatory model for why children were or were not engaged in educational computing. This tentative model helped focus the field observations and interviewing of later fieldworkers; it also provided the initial framework for the content analysis.

The seven-person team used the initial instrument to analyze one case. Extensive discussion of the similarities and differences in their analyses of this case led the team to make some modifications in the coding form. This extensive discussion also led to a consensus on the facts of that particular case, to agreement on what codes meant, and to the procedures for carrying out the remaining case analyses. The final, seventeen-page form provided space for recording more than seventy-five categories of information. (See Appendix A for more details regarding the content analysis, Appendix B for a list of major codes, and Appendix C for the coding form.)

Our research methods made possible the long-term, in-depth collection and analysis of information with frequent independent checks along the way by many people. Although time-consuming and arduous, this process has led us to put great trust in the quality of the material gathered and in our interpretation of that material for the seventy families in our investigation.

DESCRIPTION OF THE SEVENTY FAMILIES

In our comparison of the seventy families, we looked at (1) their basic demographics, (2) the presence of hardware, software, and other home technologies, and (3) types of users.

BASIC DEMOGRAPHICS

Our sample was composed of essentially white, middle-class, and upper-middle-class families located throughout the greater New York, tristate area (see Table 2.1). Occupations of fathers ranged from business executive, lawyer, and professor to magazine editor and teacher. The occupations of the few lower-middle-class fathers included electronics technician and elevator operator. A little more than a third of the mothers were full-time homemakers and the remainder worked full-time in occupations ranging from real-estate salesperson, social worker, and chef to teacher, computer programmer, waitress, and occupational therapist. Parents were for the most part in their thirties or forties. Two parents were present in nearly all of the homes.

Most of the families had one or two school-aged children. Of these school-aged boys and girls, 28 were in kindergarten through the third grade. Thirty-five were in grades four through six. Another 26 were in grades seven and eight. The remaining 38 were in grades nine through twelve. As a whole, the sample contained slightly more older boys and slightly more younger girls. Several families had infants or toddlers, and a few families had college-aged or older children who were no longer living at home. The configuration of school-aged boys and girls within families varied. Twenty-nine families had boys only. Another seventeen families had only girls. The remainder had both boys and girls. In all, our research involved 134 parents (65 fathers and 69 mothers) and 127 primary and secondary school-aged children (ages five to eighteen). (See Appendix D for a listing of the 70 families on selected demographics.)

Table 2.1. *Background Characteristics of SITE Families (N = 70)*

Characteristic	Number	Percent
Socioeconomic Status		
Upper-Middle Class	33	47
Middle Class	30	43
Lower-Middle Class	7	10
Place of Residence		
Connecticut	5	7
New Jersey	9	13
New York State (Upstate/Long Island)	19	27
New York City (All Five Boroughs)	37	53
Race		
Asian	2	3
Black	4	6
Hispanic	2	3
White	62	89
Father's Occupation		
Major Owner/Executive/Professional	30	46
Lesser Owner/Manager/Professional	23	35
Sales/Clerical/Technical	9	14
Skilled/Unskilled Labor	3	5
Mother's Day-Time Activity		
Full-Time Homemaker	23	33
Part-Time Worker	7	10
Full-Time Worker	39	56
Mother's Out-of-Home Occupation		
Major Owner/Executive/Professional	4	9
Lesser Owner/Manager/Professional	26	57
Sales/Clerical/Technical	13	28
Skilled/Unskilled Labor	3	7
Ages of Parents in the Overall Sample (N=134)		
In Their Thirties	51	38
In Their Forties	67	50
In Their Fifties	16	12

Table 2.1 (*cont.*)

Characteristic	Number	Percent
Parents Present in Each Family		
Mother and Father	64	91
Mother Only	5	7
Father Only	1	1
Number of School-Aged Children in Families		
One	27	39
Two	35	50
Three	5	7
Four or More	3	4
Sex Distribution of School-Aged Children in the Overall Sample (Ages 5 to 18: N=127)		
Boys	73	57
Girls	54	43
Sex Configuration of School-Aged Children within Families		
Boys Only	29	41
Girls Only	17	24
Boys and Girls	24	34
Grade Levels of Boys		
Kindergarten through 3rd Grade	14	19
4th through 6th Grades	20	27
7th and 8th Grades	15	21
9th through 12th Grades	24	33
Grade Levels of Girls		
Kindergarten through 3rd Grade	14	26
4th through 6th Grades	15	27
7th and 8th Grades	11	20
9th through 12th Grades	14	26

Note: Family socioeconomic status was assessed with a procedure approximating the Hollingshead Four-factor Occupational Status Scale. Because of rounding, totals do not always add up to 100 percent.

Table 2.2. *Selected Hardware Characteristics of the SITE Families (N = 70)*

Hardware Characteristic	Number	Percent
Original Purpose of Purchase		
Child's Education	32	46
Adult's Work	26	37
Work and Education	8	11
Recreation	4	6
Computers at Home		
One	51	73
More than One	19	27
Brands of Computers within Families		
Commodore	24	34
Apple	22	31
IBM	12	17
Atari	6	9
Tandy	5	7
Compaq	3	4
Macintosh	3	4
Others	11	16
Ancillary Hardware in Families		
Printer	54	77
Joystick	44	64
Modem	18	26
Mouse	11	16

Note: Under "Brands," the total percentage adds to more than 100 because some of the families had more than one kind of computer at home. Commodore models included VIC 20, Pet, and 64. Apple models included II, IIe, and IIc. "Others" included AT&T, Hyperion, Osborne, Panasonic, Texas Instruments, and Vector Graphics.

COMPUTER HARDWARE AND SOFTWARE

Nearly three-quarters of the families owned one computer (see Table 2.2). The majority had either an Apple (II, IIe, IIc) or Commodore (VIC 20, 64, or Pet). Some owned IBM PCs.

Still others had such computers as Atari, Tandy, Compaq, or Macintosh. With regard to peripherals, a large majority owned printers. Substantial proportions also possessed other ancillary hardware such as joysticks, modems, mouses, koala pads, or paddles. About half purchased their first or only machine with the education of their children upper- most in mind. More than a third did so with work as the primary motivation.

As for software, fifty-nine families had game software (see Table 2.3). The amount of game software among these families varied from a low of one or two games to a high of well over 200 games. About half of the families owned between ten and thirty packages.

Most families also had at least one word processing package. Since nearly all computers came with built-in programming software (BASIC), programming software was not listed as a separate category or included under the "other educational" category.

Nearly half of the families owned some academic software – that is, software focused on instruction in traditional areas such as math, reading, social studies, and science. However, the great majority of these families had three or four pieces at most. Only three families had ten or more pieces. Most of the academic software present in families has been characterized by those who review software as "edutainment" – subject- related software in a game format. A good example of the kind of academic software found in homes is *Math Blaster.* Adven- ture software intended to help children learn subject-related facts and logical thinking skills such as *Where in the World Is Carmen Sandiego?* was found in homes as well.

Thirty-two families had still other types of educational software. Ten had LOGO, a language often associated with graphics as well as with the learning of programming and mathematics. A handful had packages designed to help chil- dren prepare for the SATs, learn to type or draw, or use educa- tionally related electronic data bases or bulletin boards, among other things.

Table 2.3. *Presence of Types of Home Software among the SITE Families (N = 70)*

Type of Software		Number	Percent
Games	Yes	60	86
	No	10	14
Word Processing	Yes	56	80
	No	14	20
Academic	Yes	33	47
	No	37	53
Other Educational	Yes	32	46
	No	38	54
Work-related	Yes	33	47
	No	37	53
Home-related	Yes	34	49
	No	36	51

Note: Academic software includes those programs purposely designed to teach academic content whether or not they have a game format. Most of the families (21 of 33) categorized as having academic software actually had no more than three or four programs. Only several (3 of 33) had more than ten programs. Other educational software includes packages such as SAT preparation, typing, LOGO, and communications packages connecting children to educationally related electronic data bases and bulletin boards.

Nearly all computers had some form of BASIC programming software built in. Therefore, we do not present a separate category for programming nor do we include programming software under "other educational." The work-related category does not include word processing since this software is presented as a separate category above. It does include such packages as graphics and data base programs. Home-related software includes packages dealing with such topics as checkbook balancing, gardening, and address or recipe keeping.

Nearly half of the families had work-related software other than word processing. These packages most often included spreadsheets, data bases, and graphics – that is, *Visicalc, Lotus 1,2,3, dBase II or III, Appleworks, PSF File,* and *MacPaint.*

Almost half of the families had some sort of home-related software as well. These packages dealt with such topics as checkbook balancing, gardening, address keeping, or recipe storing.

OTHER HOME TECHNOLOGIES

Families differed not only in the amount and kind of computer hardware and software they owned but also in their other home technologies. A few of the families had virtually every device – electrical and mechanical – one could think of. As a member of one of these families put it: "We've thrown out more gadgets than most families ever own!" But at the time of the study none of the families had a satellite dish or a fax machine.

At the same time, some of the families were quite traditional in the purchase and use of other home technologies, preferring to go to the movies rather than buy a VCR or to use the conventional appliances for cooking rather than a microwave oven. But, as a result of their general affluence and the belief that cutting-edge domestic technologies in one way or another would make their lives at home easier, most families were amply "technologized." Typical devices in these homes were electric garage door openers; microwave ovens, Cuisinart mixers, and electric can openers and coffee makers; hand-held computers and electric pencil sharpeners; cameras and camcorders; multiple television sets with cable service, VCRs, Atari and Atari-like cartridges for TV hook-up, and stereo equipment; advanced telephones and related services; electric toothbrushes and Water Piks.

It appeared that everyone used some of these technologies – for example, the television, the phone, the stereo equipment. Our study did not establish the quantity or quality of use of these home technologies. It was not clear, for example, how sophisticated the use of the VCR was in each family. Programming it can be such a daunting experience that many people seem to shy away from it. Similarly, it is one thing to use a microwave oven to warm a cup of coffee; it is another to cook a three- or four-course meal in it. In the typical family, the home computer seemed to fit into its technological mix as the most advanced piece.

Table 2.4. *SITE Family Members According to*
Their Levels of Computer Use (N = 70)

	Level of Use	Number	Percent
PARENTS			
Total	Major	34	25
(N = 134)	Minor	40	30
	Nonuse	60	45
Fathers	Major	28	43
(N = 65)	Minor	19	29
	Nonuse	18	28
Mothers	Major	6	9
(N = 69)	Minor	21	30
	Nonuse	42	61
CHILDREN			
Total	Major	43	34
(N = 127)	Minor	63	50
	Nonuse	21	16
Sons	Major	34	47
(N = 73)	Minor	29	40
	Nonuse	10	14
Daughters	Major	9	17
(N = 54)	Minor	34	63
	Nonuse	11	20
MAJOR-USE CONFIGURATIONS	Parent(s) Only	18	26
IN FAMILIES	Child(ren) Only	22	31
	Parent and Child	14	20
	No Major Use	16	23

Note: Major users worked on the computer regularly for some continuing purpose or purposes important to them. They would typically use it for long stretches many days a week. Minor users were not really interested in using the computer to accomplish tasks. Some used it sporadically, others almost never. Nonusers completely ignored computers at home.

TYPES OF USERS AT HOME

In our study there were seventy-seven major users – that is, people who used their machines hours at a time and regularly during the week, if not every day, for completing tasks important to them (see Table 2.4). Of the major users, forty-three were children and thirty-four were parents. A much greater number of fathers were major users compared with mothers. Similarly, sons were far more likely to be major users than daughters.

Family configurations of major users were somewhat evenly distributed. Eighteen of the families had parent-only major users. In twenty-two of the families at least one major user was a child. Fourteen of the families had at least one parent *and* one child as major users. Sixteen families had no major users.

Families frequently had one or more minor users – that is, people who used the computer sporadically for tasks they perceived as important. A large majority of daughters fell into this category, as did a smaller proportion of sons.

A large percentage of mothers were nonusers – that is, people who did not know how to use the computer or, if they knew how, did not use it anyway. It should be noted that some fathers, daughters, and sons were also nonusers, although in far smaller proportions than mothers.

THE REPRESENTATIVENESS OF SITE FAMILIES

The SITE families were not selected in a scientifically random manner, as might have been done in a national survey. Nevertheless, except for location, the characteristics of SITE families parallel those of the larger population of primarily middle- and upper-middle-class American families with children who had purchased home computers at the time of the study (see, e.g., Hoban, 1985; Simonsen and Hessel, 1985; and Taylor, 1985). Moreover, the evidence we have seen since then (e.g., Depke, 1990; Scott, Cole, and Engel, 1992) convinces us that the profiles of families purchasing computers for their school-aged children *today* are quite similar to those in our study.[4]

NOTES

1. Differences between these two broad research approaches can be related to their purpose, design, and analysis. Specific types of quantitative research designs include experiments, quasi experiments, and survey research. Qualitative research comes in a variety of shapes, including case study designs, ethnography, participant observation, and phenomenology.

2. At that time, the differences in the number and quality of studies of home educational computing compared with school computing were very large. Since then, these differences have merely increased. Because of its size and researcher interests, the literature on school computing has divided into many specialized areas. The research literature on children's educational computing at home, however, has remained undifferentiated and minuscule. Part of the reason may result from the difficulties of studying behavior in families. Family settings are private places, unlike schools, which are public places. Researchers have difficulty – even when their incentive is strong – gaining entrance into homes for even brief periods, let alone for longer periods. In addition, the labor-intensive quality of such investigations makes their "costs" prohibitive. One notable exception is the promising work of Margalit (1990) on the use of home computers for the education of disabled children in Israel. Earlier published work on family educational computing in the United States includes that of Gottlieb and Dede (1983), Sussman (1985), McKnight (1986), and Ancarrow (1987).

3. During the past decade or so, the qualitative approach has expanded greatly. The SITE study combined basic qualitative designs, as do many qualitative studies. For recent overviews of qualitative research, see Bogdan and Biklen (1992), Glesne and Peshkin (1992), Miles and Huberman (1984), Platt (1992), and Strauss and Corbin (1990).

4. It is true that there are new or ongoing school experiments or projects in various parts of the country that assign home computers, often to lower-middle-class and lower-class families – for example, Apple's ACOT Project, Indiana's Buddy Project, and New York City's Project Tell. These and others will be discussed in Chapter 11. While it is difficult to estimate the absolute number of students touched by experiments and projects such as these, the number is extremely small in comparison with the

many millions of families, largely middle- and upper-middle-class, who currently have home computers. So, the *overall* picture of what is happening in families in the name of academic computing would not be altered even if these experimental families were added to the mix. Parenthetically, we think that rigorous research of these "experimental" families in all likelihood would confirm the dominant role played by the school in a child's academic efforts at home, a fact that some proponents of home academic computing had hoped would be offset by family purchases of home computers for children's learning.

Chapter 3

The Absence of Children's Academic Computing at Home

I guess if I felt they were wasting time playing games while they were having problems in school, I'd probably want them to use the computer for educational purposes. Right now I don't really care if they just use it to play games because they're both doing fine in school. (A SITE mother of two boys, one fourteen and the other eleven years old)

The simple fact that families purchase computers says next to nothing about their actual uses and the reasons why. The parents or children in nearly all seventy families we studied were, in fact, using their home computers. These machines, for the most part, were not gathering dust in corners or closets. Within the families that bought this technology primarily or secondarily for education, however, the children were not using their computers by and large for educational purposes, especially for academic computing.[1] The reasons include the lack of parental encouragement and assistance; school emphasis, if at all, on other forms of computing; and children's lack of interest in using computers for education.

In this chapter, we describe the kinds of home computing parents and children performed in general, and we identify four types of families. We tabulate our findings concerning children's minimal academic use in all seventy families and present a qualitative comparison of four selected families. We also present an explanatory model for academic computing containing these conditions and their interrelationships.

PARENTAL HOME COMPUTING EFFORTS

In over half of the families at least one parent – predominantly but not exclusively fathers – used their home computers for work-related purposes (see Table 3.1). Of these parents, the majority engaged in work-related computing on a regular basis – that is, at least two or three times a week. Others were more sporadic, often engaging in computing less than once a week. While work-related computing involved primarily the word processing of memos and other business correspondence, some spreadsheet analysis, data base analysis, and telecommunications also occurred.

In about a third of the families at least one parent was engaged in home computing, usually for a single purpose such as recreation or home management or adult education. A few – primarily fathers – used their computers for recreation, mainly game playing. Several mothers used their computers for home-management purposes such as putting recipes or address/phonebooks on disk. One mother had a piece of software that allowed her to plot a vegetable garden. A few parents, usually mothers, wrote letters to friends on their computers or typed school papers for their children. One parent was learning keyboarding, and another was studying a foreign language on the computer.

In a quarter of the families, parents used their computers for both work and home purposes. Although use for work purposes could be characterized as ardent, for home purposes it was casual and infrequent. In contrast, parents in a third of the families did not engage in any kind of computing.

CHILDREN'S HOME COMPUTING EFFORTS

Children used the home computers in much greater proportions than their parents. Primarily, they played games. Some did programming or word processing.

THE PLAYING OF GAMES

Without doubt, the children-preferred computing activity was game playing.[2] In over three-quarters of the families children

31

Table 3.1. *Home Computing Activities of SITE Families*
(N = 70)

Activity	Amount	Number	Percent
CHILDREN			
Game Playing	Much	23	33
	Some	16	23
	Little	16	23
	None	15	21
Programming	Much	9	13
	Some	10	14
	Little	13	19
	None	38	54
Word Processing	Much	7	10
	Some	13	19
	Little	12	17
	None	38	54
PARENTS			
Work-related	Much	25	36
	Some	9	13
	Little	6	9
	None	30	43
Home-related	Two or More Areas	6	9
	One Area	19	27
	None	45	64
Combinations of Activities	Home and Work	18	26
	Home Only	7	10
	Work Only	21	30
	No Parental Use	24	34

engaged to varying degrees in the playing of games. Indeed, many were unwilling to use their computers for anything else even though they had been exposed to other uses at school, primarily through programming and computer literacy classes. Those who used their computers for other purposes often remained dedicated game players as well. In fifteen families, on the other hand, children did not play computer games, some because their parents would not allow it, some because they were too young, and some – mainly girls – because they themselves were not interested or did not like the kinds of gameware available.

WORD PROCESSING AND PROGRAMMING

Children in almost half of the families were making an effort to do some programming or word processing. A few did so on a weekly basis, but most did not. Children in over half of the families did no programming or word processing.

Although the quality of programming or word processing was not the focus of this research, impressions from the field strongly suggest that the quality was on average low. For example, only a handful of children in our sample were using home computers to learn how to write. More typically, these machines were used as sophisticated typewriters.[3]

Programming at home was largely in response to school homework assignments or the challenge of creating or modifying games obtained from magazines and friends. More often than not, these efforts appeared to be rudimentary at best. Nevertheless, a few children approached "hacker" status.[4] One, for example, was engaged in what appeared to be advanced programming using a language such as Pascal.

OTHER FORMS OF COMPUTING

Other forms of educational and quasi-educational computing were engaged in less frequently. Some children with typing software sometimes worked on their keyboarding skills. Others with graphics packages occasionally created images for school papers or, in a more recreational mode, spent time at home drawing. Several high schoolers were using or had used

Table 3.2. *SITE Families Grouped According to Children's Academic Computing at Home and the Presence of Academic Software (N = 70)*

Classification	Number	Percent
Type I Families:		
No academic computing or academic software present	36	51
Type II Families:		
No academic computing but academic software present	21	30
Type III Families:		
Sporadic or irregular academic computing with academic software	12	17
Type IV Families:		
Ongoing, regular academic computing with academic software	1	1

Note: The total is less than 100 percent because of rounding.

special packages to prepare for the Scholastic Aptitude Test. One or two attempted to compose melodies with music software. Several with modems and the necessary software accessed electronic bulletin boards once in a while to obtain information for school assignments or for personal purposes.

Although varying kinds of educational home computing did take place, most efforts, when they did occur, were not very serious or consistent. Indeed, there was much less educational activity than one might have expected given the software packages available or present in the homes. In other words, while the machines were not gathering dust, a lot of software was not being used, especially that for academic learning.

THE MINIMAL ACADEMIC COMPUTING EFFORTS OF CHILDREN AT HOME

On the basis of data from fieldworker logs and analytic papers, we classified families into four types according to whether they had academic software and whether at least one child was using it. Type I consisted of thirty-six families in which no children were engaged in academic computing and there was no academic software (see Table 3.2). Type II was made up of another twenty-one families, or roughly a third of the study group. In this type, academic software was present in the home, but children were not engaged in academic computing.

Of those that remained, twelve were Type III families, that is, those in which at least one child was using academic software sporadically or irregularly. Type IV consisted of one family, in which a sister and her slightly younger brother, both in elementary school, were engaged in the regular use of various academic software packages purchased specifically for this purpose by their mother.

In short, our analysis demonstrated that children's academic computing was missing in four-fifths of the families and was minimal in nearly all the others.

FACTORS AFFECTING CHILDREN'S ACADEMIC COMPUTING EFFORTS

Field observations and the reports of fieldworkers indicated that the extent of children's academic computing efforts at home could be attributed to several factors: (1) parental encouragement and assistance, (2) school emphasis, (3) peer pressure,[5] (4) sibling support, (5) the presence of suitable software and hardware, (6) a child's earlier computer experiences, and (7) current child receptivity.

TRENDS ACROSS THE SEVENTY FAMILIES

As one moves across the four types of families, the prevalence of a condition tends to increase (Table 3.3). For example, parental encouragement and assistance was observed in less than one-quarter of Type I and Type II families, while it was found in more than a quarter of Type III homes. Therefore, Type I and Type II families, as groups, were judged to be "low" on this condition, while the group of Type III families was assessed as

Table 3.3. *Conditions Directly Influencing Children's Academic Computing at Home (N = 70)*

	Family Classification			
Condition	I (N = 36)	II (N = 21)	III (N = 12)	IV (N = 1)
1. Parental encouragement for and aid with academic computing	L	L	ML	H
2. School emphasis on academic computing	L	L	L	H
3. Peer pressure for academic computing	L	L	L	ML
4. Sibling support for academic computing	L	L	L	ML
5. Presence of hardware and academic software at home	L	L	M	H
6. Early positive academic computing experiences	L	L	ML	H
7. Child receptivity to academic computing	L	L	ML	M

Note: Family Classification: I = no academic computing or academic software at home; II = no academic computing at home but academic software is present; III = sporadic or irregular academic computing at home; IV = regular, ongoing academic computing at home. Ratings: low (L)= fewer than one-quarter of the families in a given classification evidenced the condition; moderately low (ML) = fewer than one-half of the families evidenced the condition; moderate (M) = one-half to three-quarters showed its presence; and high (H) = more than three-quarters evidenced its presence.

"moderately low." Because of the strong pressure and support for academic computing in the one Type IV family, this type was assessed as "high."

Child receptivity to academic computing was assessed as "low" for Type I and Type II families since it was observed in fewer than one-quarter of these homes. Child receptivity for

Type III families was judged "moderately low" because it was present in more than a quarter of these homes but not quite half. In the case of the Type IV family, its presence was "moderate." While both children in this family had positive feelings about their academic computing, they did express some reservations about making such regular efforts in all of the subject areas required by their mother.[6] Similarly positive trends are also apparent for the other five conditions.

When the findings across the groups are compared, both Type I and Type II families (homes in which no academic computing was occurring) had "low" ratings on all seven conditions. Type III families (in which sporadic academic computing was present) had three "low" ratings, three "moderately low" ratings, and one "moderate" rating. The Type IV family had no "low" ratings, two "moderately low" ratings, one "moderate" rating, and four "high" ratings.

A FOUR-FAMILY QUALITATIVE COMPARISON

The above analysis deals with these seven conditions individually. It says little about their interplay. How these factors came together in real families can be seen in the experience of the Smith, the Green, the Redd, and the Quarles families, each of which represents one of the four family types.[7]

The *Smiths* were a *Type I family:* neither their sixteen-year-old daughter nor their thirteen-year-old son engaged in academic computing at home. They had no academic software. Mr. Smith, in his fifties, was a telephone technician. Mrs. Smith, also in her fifties, worked at a local coffee shop.

The Smiths had a Commodore 64 and an AT&T 6300, the latter given to Mr. Smith after he took a company-sponsored training course. The AT&T had a printer, a modem, and several pieces of business and recreational software.

Mr. Smith was the dominant user, especially for work purposes, but his opinion of educational computing for his children was negative:

> I'll be honest with you. I'm against computers . . . because eventually they are going to make you a dumb person, O.K.? If

you have kids on a computer at an early age, they are not going to learn how to spell [or how] to write. . . . They may not know they made an error if the computer will do it for them.

Mrs. Smith was a nonuser, but she seemed more positive: "Well what is the purpose of having a computer?" She then conjectured, "Using it for reading is very good. I could use the computer to learn a new skill, such as a foreign language." Mr. Smith, however, indicated that learning such subjects would mean getting the software and "that's a lot of money!"

Their daughter described her effort to write up a chemistry assignment on the Commodore as "fruitless." She maintained that it was better for her to use books to learn her lessons. Nevertheless, she thought that academic computing at home could help her brother with *his* schoolwork. But the brother refused to use either machine for anything but occasional programming or the playing of games. Neither was asked to do academic computing at school. An English teacher was teaching the son's computer course because no one else was available. According to the son, "She doesn't know what she's doing."

The *Greens* were a *Type II family:* neither their seventeen-year-old son nor their ten-year-old daughter was engaged in academic computing at home. Their seven pieces of academic software had been purchased earlier "when the children were younger," and according to them, "it was no longer suitable." Mr. Green was a marketing consultant in his early forties. Mrs. Green, also in her early forties, was a part-time library assistant.

The family owned an Apple II+, a printer, joystick, modem, and a great deal of game and business software. Unlike the Smith father, Mr. Green initially purchased the computer for his children because he wanted to expose them to it early on. As he put it: "If they got a feel for the computer, even if only through games and typing at first, they would have an edge later in school." Nevertheless, he became the major user, regularly bringing work home from the office to do on it.

Mrs. Green, a nonuser, was opposed to buying a computer: "I was against it. It was his idea and he went out himself and bought it at some warehouse. I was against it because of the money, but he was convinced it was the thing of the future."

The son's programming course at school involved mainly games. He used the home computer only to get together to copy and trade games with his friends. The daughter's school was using computers in reading and math labs for "drill and skill" exercises, but her class was not. She once used the home computer to try to improve her reading skills but stopped out of dislike. At the time of the fieldwork, she preferred playing with her friends on their Atari game machine. Now away at college, an older daughter abandoned the computer when she was younger and living at home after discovering that it would not "automatically" do her math homework.

The *Redds* were a *Type III family:* their two sons – fourteen and ten – used their Apple IIe computer sporadically for academics. They had four pieces of academic software that were math or reading related. Mr. Redd, in his fifties, was a top executive of a business firm. Mrs. Redd, just shy of fifty, was a devoted homemaker who had just gone back to work as a part-time clerk/typist.

Mr. Redd was an avid business user of their Apple IIe and printer, which he had purchased primarily for himself and secondarily for his older son, who was having learning difficulties at school. He had also just bought a Macintosh saying, "I just wanted it so I could learn more powerful [business] programs." Mrs. Redd, on the other hand, would have nothing to do with either computer. She did not want to use computers, did not like them, and simply avoided them despite the fact that learning how to word process might have helped her at work. As she said: "I never touch the Apple."

Mr. Redd maintained that he lived by the maxim: "Life is not a book to be read, but a page to be written." However, he took a hands-off approach when it came to his sons' school achievement:

> Kids must be self-motivating. Parents can't push them into things. Once they see what they like, they'll do it. It is better to have them happy and happy-go-lucky than to sit on them. . . . A

child has to be self-motivated. A parent can't push him into using the micro, for the child will never stick to it. . . . We haven't used the computer to demand excellence from the kids.

Mrs. Redd's educational approach was similar. When her younger son came home one day and asked what she and her husband would do if he got a "D" on his report card, she replied that they "would do nothing." About computers, she said, "Kids will always be more interested in the games, not the educational software." Her younger son clearly fell into this camp.

The Redds perceived their neighbors and friends as being "sometimes openly hostile" to their owning of computers. Moreover, both boys' teachers seemed to discourage computer use for homework. One son's teacher had told him: "It isn't fair for you to use your Apple! Other children's families can't afford them."

The older son who used their math and English software sporadically for drill indicated that he had "not needed to do that lately." He maintained that he did not care about computers and neither did his friends. When Mrs. Redd said she wished he would spend more time using the computer, Mr. Redd interrupted: "Why should he use it when he doesn't need it? He doesn't think he needs it!" At the end of the fieldwork, the younger boy began to falter in school while the older boy began to make academic gains. Both parents seemed bewildered. "None of this is because of me or my wife. We are doing what we always do with the boys [academically], nothing."

The *Quarles* were a *Type IV family:* both their twelve-year-old daughter and eleven-year-old son were engaged in regular academic computing at home. They had many pieces of academic software. In his forties, Dr. Quarles was a physician. Mrs. Quarles, in her late thirties, was a well educated full-time homemaker. At the time of the study, she was learning how to program and word process on their Apple IIe in order to computerize her husband's billing of patients and other office activities. Dr. Quarles refused to have anything personally to do with computers.

The son, when asked if he was still on the schedule his mother had put him and his sister on, said: "You'd better believe it, and now [since their mother had recently bought Apple IIc computers for both of them] we have almost twice as much time on the computer." He explained somewhat unhappily that he still had to do his spelling, reading, and math practice before he could play games on his computer. As to whether his mother had asked him if he wanted his own computer, he replied: "No, she just told us we would be getting the computers and we would be using them in our rooms and they would be ours."

The daughter was not kept on a schedule like her brother. She still had to do her drill and practice every day, but she was permitted to set the time. The computer in her room often had a box, which matched the wallpaper, over it. When asked why she kept the box over her computer, she answered that she did not want to see the "big green eye staring" at her when she was not using it.

Much but not all of the daughter's software was related to math. Her newest program was on simple algebra, which she was taking in school. She felt that algebra practice on the computer was helpful to her except that there were times when the program's explanation was different from that of the teacher. When this happens, she said, "I forget what the computer explains." She also felt that while the computer was helping her in math, it was not helping in the subjects she liked best: reading and art.

Mrs. Quarles was pleased with her children's progress in school, believing strongly that it was due to their computer use at home. She explained that "[despite] the school and its good teachers, good programs, and administration, parents still need to assume responsibility for their children's learning in all their subject areas." Mrs. Quarles was in regular contact with her children's teachers and with the computer-lab coordinator to find out what subjects the kids were covering, get copies of the reading and math curricula, find out what progress they were making in their classes, and determine their weaknesses.

Mrs. Quarles was also active at her children's school. As she remarked: "I am involved in some of the activities [fund-raising and school publications] at the kids' school. So, whenever I am there, I make it my business to speak to the teachers, especially the media person, since this is a major part of her role."

The school had a minicomputer and, in addition to programming, emphasized computer-assisted instruction, especially reading and math in the intermediate grades. The primary grades received instruction in computer awareness and LOGO. The intermediates had math and reading and maybe LOGO and BASIC as well, depending upon the teacher. The teachers used printout diagnostics from the computer to aid children and to inform other teachers and the parents. The media director confirmed Mrs. Quarles's school involvement:

> Most of the parents who ask for information [about software] are parents that are involved in some way with the school. There are a group of parents who perceive their kids' education as vital . . . vital to the point that they [the parents] are preparing the kids at this time for college. Mrs. Quarles is usually in the thick of things here at the school.

The above portraits make clear the extent of academic computing occurring in these four homes and the conditions surrounding children's efforts or lack thereof. Clearly, neither the Smiths (Type I) nor the Greens (Type II) were utilizing their computers educationally. Though sporadic, there was some current use by the Redds (Type III). In contrast, both Quarles (Type IV) children were regular, ongoing users.

Real parental encouragement and assistance were absent in the first three families. It seems ironic that the three fathers who were computer competent gave little or no help or encouragement to their children and in some ways actively discouraged the academic use of the computer. It is more understandable why the mothers in the Smith, Green, and Redd families did not, since they were essentially computer avoiders. By contrast, in the Quarles family it was the father who would have nothing to do with computers. Here, it was the computer-competent mother who encouraged and aided her children and who proactively sought advice from her children's school about appropriate software.

On the other hand, all the Smith, Green, and Redd parents appeared distanced from the schools their children attended, especially when it came to computers. The schools, except for the one attended by the Quarles children, stressed other forms of computer use, often in an inadequate manner or, in the Redd's case, actively discouraged its use for completing homework assignments. The Smith and Green children had largely poor earlier experiences with computers at school and home and were essentially unwilling to continue trying. For this and other reasons, these children seemed to have an aversion to educational computing. The Redd son was self-motivated but only when he ran into learning *problems.* While the Quarles children were working on their home computers, they did not appear all that eager to do so. Siblings and peers were more desirous of playing games; they did not encourage or help each other use their computers for academics. This seemed true in all four families.

A MODEL OF CONDITIONS AFFECTING ACADEMIC COMPUTING

The above family sketches suggest that the seven conditions form an interrelated network of forces impacting on children's academic computing efforts. The relations among these conditions and their antecedents are taken up in more detail in subsequent chapters. For now, we present our general model.

This model (see Figure 3.1) posits that children's lack of home effort is primarily due to their parents' lack of encouragement and assistance. Instead of offering their support – something hoped for by some reformers – parents make little effort to search for and purchase suitable educational software. In the absence of such parental support, children are encouraged to resist learning academics at home.

43

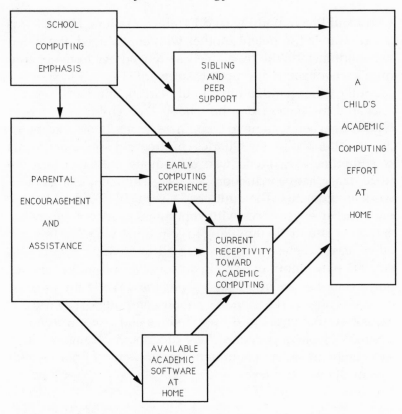

Figure 3.1. A matrix of factors influencing a child's academic computing effort at home.

A child's resistance may come also from a lack of earlier positive computer experiences having to do with the learning of academics. Many children have negative computer experiences in school if, indeed, they have them at all. Unless children are falling behind or have low grades, schools tend to expose them to other forms of computing, such as programming and computer literacy, a pattern that continues in most schools. Moreover, the school has an indirect effect on children's home efforts by signaling that parents' encouragement of home *academic* computing is not important. This message probably sits well with the majority of parents because they want or take educational direction from the schools. "If the schools aren't doing it or asking for it, why should we?" The school has a direct negative effect on home academic computing by not exposing children to computer-related instruction in their classrooms and by not requiring that homework assignments be done on the computer.

Along with these factors, the lack of sibling and peer support of home educational efforts on the computer further contributes to children's lack of receptivity. Children's lack of receptivity, in turn, helps explain why many children make little or no effort to utilize their computers at home for academics nor urge their parents to help them in such efforts.[8]

In summary, this chapter has shown that many children in our study were engaged in playing games on their home computers and to a far lesser degree in some forms of educational computing. Academic computing was minimal or missing. Moreover, this near absence flowed from a set of interrelated home and school forces. In the next several chapters, we deal in greater detail with these conditions and their antecedents. We turn first to the condition that is perhaps most often used as the reason for children's lack of academic computing efforts: the availability of suitable educational software.

NOTES

1. Again, by academic computing we mean children's computer use for learning such subjects and skills as mathematics, reading, science, social studies, writing, and critical thinking.
2. Data released by Nintendo of America, Inc. and reported by Michael Lev in the *New York Times* (April 29, 1990, p. 10F) show that during the period of the SITE study there was a great dip in Nintendo software purchases. This dip was dramatic: going from a high of over $3 billion in 1982 to just about $100 million in 1985. Clearly, part of the reason for this dip was the growing interest among children in the playing of games on their home computers and the rigorous development of game software for personal computers during this period. This dip happened during the period of the study and so it is little wonder that we found game

playing on home computers so strong among SITE children. However, Nintendo started to rebound in 1986 and by 1990 was projected to have annual sales of over $5 billion. And, given the new wave of 16-bit machines by Nintendo and other manufacturers, it would not be surprising to find that their 1992 sales have exceeded such earlier projections (Ferrell, 1989). See also Lewis (1989), McGill (1989), and Rothstein (1990). One implication is that today in families similar to those in the SITE study, children are for the most part not using their home computers for game playing, preferring separate game systems like Nintendo or Sega. Another possible implication is that the home computer use of children, except for the word processing of school papers, might actually be at an all-time low. The need for further research in this area is clear.

3. There is nothing wrong with this, and children can learn about writing and revising in this way. Indeed, this may well represent a first step toward using computers for composing text and for revising. In itself, however, this kind of word processing does not focus on learning how to write or how to revise one's writing. Therefore, although "educational," we would consider this kind of computer use as being minimally so.

4. The child who came closest to hacker status was Ken Darrow, a thirteen-year-old who had become interested in computing because of his earlier programming experiences at school. But Ken was not attracted to the use of computers for academic learning. He thought that if one was having problems at school then maybe academic computing might be valuable. At the time of the study, he preferred to engage in a variety of activities including word processing, programming, and the playing of sophisticated games. He was the most active among a handful of children in the study who used their computers for telecommunicating. His parents – both nonusers – had bought a modem and had installed a separate phone line for his use. Ken's parents differed on the value of his computer involvement. Mr. Darrow said, "In a way it [the computer] has given Ken a focus that I encourage." Mrs. Darrow was not as certain about its effects on Ken. As Mr. Darrow pointed out to the fieldworker: "Mrs. D. will be the first to say that Ken's [skin] looks like cream cheese, some Saturday morning when the sun is shining and he is in the house [using his computer]."

5. In this book, we use such terms as "encouragement," "emphasis," "support," and "pressure" interchangeably. We do not place a

negative connotation on "pressure," while recognizing that some authors restrict the meaning of this word to the "forcing" of someone against their will to try something. For us, all of these terms have the connotation of "inducing." For a similar meaning in the general area of planned change, see Huberman and Miles (1984). The fundamental idea is that one person is verbally trying to get another to try something or make an effort to behave or think in a certain way. Moreover, the idea often implies that the expression of the desire to get somebody to do something is backed up with some sort of behavior(s) meant to get or assist the other person to act in the desired way. In our case, this meant getting a child to use the computer at home in order to learn academics.

6. A moderate assessment for any other group – e.g., the presence of home academic software for Type III families – meant that the condition was present in half to three-quarters of the families. An assessment of high on a condition for the other groups would have required its presence in more than three-quarters of the families in that group.

7. Some of the facts about the Smiths and Greens were presented in an earlier article (Giacquinta and Lane, 1990). Material about the Redd and Quarles families is contained in an earlier unpublished document (Giacquinta and Ely, 1986).

8. This model maps out pathways whereby seven factors influenced the academic computing efforts of children at home. It is important to note that not all families were subjected to all of the conditions in exactly the same way. Even though these seven conditions touched all families to one degree or another, in some families, one or two of these factors or pathways dominated; in other families, still others of the factors and pathways appeared more salient.

Chapter 4

The Availability of Educational
Software

> It is software more so than computers themselves that will ul-
> timately determine whether educational computing will have a
> long-term future and reach its instructional potential. (Williams
> and Williams, 1985, p. 5)

Perhaps more has been written about software than any other
topic in educational computing. At the time of our study, many
observers held that existing academic or educational software
led children to engage in nothing more than "electronic page
turning." Others argued that while most software was inadequate, useful packages did exist.

The literature on software at the time of our study convinced
us that the bulk of commercially developed instructional software did have serious limitations. It also indicated that a good
deal of software was useful, and that educational computing
in the home was worthwhile for children. We therefore concluded that there were far fewer Type III and Type IV families
than Type I and Type II families *not* because of the *unavailability*
of good software. Instead, the reasons, then and now, have
more to do with family educational practices, family
knowledge and attitudes about software and computers in
general, and the conditions shaping families' knowledge, attitudes, and practices.

In this chapter we look closer at the quality and quantity
of academic software present within the families in our
sample and compare the results with observations about
software in the literature. We then show how family awareness and appraisals of software affected the presence or ab-

sence of software and its use when present. We also raise some hardware and ergonomic issues contributing to software usage at home. We end the chapter with a brief look at what has happened to instructional software since our study.

EXISTING EDUCATIONAL SOFTWARE

By 1984, market research experts, professional reviewers, and other observers of the software scene seemed to agree that the educational software market was vast. Well known among these experts is Ken Komoski, executive director of the Educational Products Information Exchange Institute (EPIE), arguably the most thorough educational software evaluation institution in the United States. Komoski (1984, p. 247) estimated that there were seven to ten thousand commercially produced educational packages in the country at that time, and that only 5 percent was of "truly high quality."[1] More than half was judged "not worth recommending to educators or parents."[2]

Perhaps in part to counter manufacturers' exaggerated claims about software, Komoski emphasized that a lot of this software was not even worth trying out in schools or homes. Actually, EPIE had found – albeit with some reservation – that three or four out of every ten programs were recommendable and that the amount qualifying for this "recommended" rating had risen from 27 to 35 percent in just one year. Komoski (1984, p. 248) himself stated: "This is not to say that excellent software programs do not exist. They most certainly do. But, for a number of reasons, many of today's high-quality programs may be unknown to school and home consumers." He attributed this lack of awareness in part to the fact that (1) the "glut of glowing advertising campaigns for *all* [emphasis in original] software" masks the truly good packages, and (2) some of the best software comes from companies that cannot afford to spread knowledge about their products across large numbers of consumers (p. 248).

Other observers noted that the vast array of programs may have caused more frustration than sense of opportunity for parents and teachers who had to evaluate the packages for use with their children. Williams and Williams (1985, p. 7) wrote that "software is being produced far faster than many educators can keep up with," and Watkins and Brimm (1985, pp. 142–3) observed that the "experience of searching for computer materials is overwhelming, even for a computer-wise scholar."

In a study for the Carnegie Corporation, Marc Tucker, another observer of educational technology, also concluded that "good software" did exist, "although not in great supply" ("From Drill Sergeant," 1985, p. 2).[3] Of this good software, he went on to say:

> One kind is pedagogical – intended to teach concepts or subject matter. Another is productivity, or tool, software – such as word processing, data-base management systems, computer graphics, spreadsheets, and models and simulations – aimed at enhancing intellectual and problem-solving capability.

THE QUALITY OF SOFTWARE PRESENT
IN HOMES

Earlier in the book we reported that nearly half of the SITE families possessed some academic software. With some overlap of titles, the absolute total came to over 150 pieces. Some of these were of the drill and practice kind; others were tutorial in nature; and, still others were simulations. The majority were gamelike in format. If the other kinds of educational software are included – for example, that dealing with the development of critical thinking or fostering a knowledge of music, art, keyboarding, prereading skills and programming – the number exceeds 200.[4]

The software fell into several categories: (1) early or preschool (e.g., *Facemaker, Gertrude's Secrets, Kindercomp, Stickybear-ABC, Stickybear-Opposites*); (2) language arts (e.g., *Apple Grammar, Jotto, M–ss–ng L–nks, Reading Comprehension, Way to Read Words,*

Word Quest); and (3) mathematics (e.g., *Algebra, Fraction Teacher, Lemonade, Math Applesoft, Math Blaster, Math City, Mathware, Pie and Line Graphs, Snoopy Math, Speed/Bingo Math, Space Math, Trig Function/Acute Angle).* Other pieces of software included *Bank Street Writer, Clock, Dungeons & Dragons, The Factory, Logo Design, Music Composer, Master Type, Rocky's Boots, SAT Verbal Drill, Snooper Troops, Turtle, Typing Tutor, Where in the World Is Carmen Sandiego?*

What was the quality of this software? In assessing it, we relied on the work of EPIE reported in *The Educational Software Selector* (TESS). EPIE used a four-tiered rating system for software: "highly recommended," "recommended with reservations," "not recommended but may meet some needs," and "do not consider" (EPIE, 1985, p. 6). Of the academic software present in SITE families, 6 percent was categorized in TESS as "highly recommended" and another 33 percent as "recommended with reservations." Only 8 percent fell into the "not recommended but may meet some needs" category. None fell into the "do not consider" category. Another 38 percent was listed in TESS but had not been evaluated. The remaining 14 percent was unlisted.

The above findings and analysis led us to two conclusions: that a considerable amount of decent software was available for home use and that some of it was present in families in our study. What, then, stopped families from getting it and using it? The answer lies mainly in the perceptions of the parents and children.

FAMILY PERCEPTIONS OF EDUCATIONAL SOFTWARE

Family members themselves provided key reasons for the absence or lack of use of educational software. Many knew next to nothing about educational software. Others, who were aware and knowledgeable, did not perceive available software to be "worthwhile," thought it was "too expensive," or saw it as "inappropriate" for *their* children.

INSUFFICIENT KNOWLEDGE AND
AWARENESS

Most parents in our study knew little about the extant software for educational computing. Typical was the comment: "I don't know anything about it." Many reported that they had not kept up with current developments: "You know, we've had a computer for five years. We bought the software back then, and it wasn't very sophisticated, and we just never tried it again." In addition, parents reported that retailers and sales-people were not satisfactory resources:

> The computer stores are not particularly helpful in this regard since the descriptions on the disk packages really don't explain what the disk contains, and the salespeople only have a general idea. . . . It would be great if they had sample disks in the store; then you could try different programs and decide which was best. There's no way of previewing a program before you buy it. . . . I don't want to buy something and then find that it will not serve the purpose.

The most knowledgeable parents indicated that their best sources for information were computer magazines, software evaluations, or recommendations of friends and school.

THE LOW OPINION OF
EDUCATIONAL SOFTWARE

A large group of parents stated that they viewed the existing educational software as "not worthwhile." They commented on content flaws, difficult-to-follow directions and documentation, and "bugs" in the program that caused software to be unusable. They expressed dissatisfaction with instructional design features, the lack of sophisticated concepts, and a failure of software to exploit the interactive potential of the computer. Three comments from parents illustrate this dissatisfaction:

> The educational software is too prosaic and not stimulating enough.

> You can't find anything that's intermediate math. . . . Current educational programs, tutorials, for the computer for Vincent

and Mary are too basic. . . . They are just adding and subtracting. . . . Educational programs are not sophisticated enough to help a student who is past the sixth grade.

Educational software is to teaching what TV is to recreation . . . mindless!

Some parents were critical of instructional design features, and characterized educational software as "elaborate workbooks," "flat and noninteractive," and "glorified textbooks." They commented:

Educational software? To me, about 90 percent of it is garbage. All it is is a workbook using a screen. . . . It's not interactive. It asks you a question, and you answer the question. . . . You don't need a machine for that. . . . To me, that's a misuse of it.

Commercial packages used for drills. . . . those are like electronic flashcards which do not really teach anything but babysitting.

The SAT stuff is very inadequate. I saw one . . . for $50 and all it consisted of was 300 vocabulary words. Big deal. Give them a book! Why do you need a machine for that?

Children, too, criticized design features of software they encountered at school. The following two reactions were typical: "Most school software is dumb. Who wants to shoot a guy when you get something right? It's dumb!" and "I used the software, but once you've done it, there's no point in doing it again – it's also very tedious to do."

As noted earlier, the most prevalent software found in homes was game software. For parents, as well as for software developers, the boundaries between education and entertainment frequently blurred into "edutainment" software that used a game format to teach rudimentary skills. Williams and Williams (1985) noted that much of the educational software evolved from game software and capitalized on the production characteristics of games by making the context of instruction gamelike. One mother commented:

53

"Onceyou'veplayed it, it stays the same." Few parents made any attempt to find out how to locate software for their children, and they spent little time exploring the quality of specific packages:

> We've never really planned or looked into educational software. Toy stores don't carry the really "heavy stuff."

> I've heard of educational software but I don't think any of it is any good yet. And I'm not holding my breath waiting for some to be developed!

THE HIGH COST

For some, educational software was simply too expensive to try out, especially given its assumed weaknesses:

> He said that educational software is not popular, and he doesn't buy any because in the first place, it's too expensive.

> She said that the reason she hasn't purchased any educational software directly was the cost and that she would rent them if there was a convenient local place from which to do so.

> Well, they are expensive, even if we did get a good price for them – probably not worth the money – no, I don't think John would use them enough.

THE DEFICIENCY ASSUMPTION

Many parents thought that educational software was useful primarily for drill and practice in basic skill development, especially for those with school-related deficiencies. As one parent put it, "Educational software is for people who are having trouble. It's remedial. It's corrective." Another commented, "It is more appropriate for very young children learning basic skills or for those who are learning disabled." And still a third said, "The boys haven't really needed any [educational] software, and they've never asked for any so we've never bought any."

THE COMPATIBILITY OF
HOME HARDWARE

Another important constraint on a family's purchase and use of educational software was, and perhaps still is, the compatibility of their hardware with educational software. Many parents who had purchased a computer for their business needs found that the educational software they were interested in for their children was not written for their machine. Many also found that their home computer was not compatible with those at their children's schools or with the software being used there.[5] Some families saw quickly that more than one home computer configuration was necessary – one for educational purposes and a different one for professional uses. This translated into an expensive undertaking for most families.

Unfortunately, many of the problems with the purchase of compatible hardware encountered in the mid-1980s still prevail. Today, the purchase of a home computer may be even a more daunting experience for families. There is a wider range of manufacturers and stores selling computers; there are more options and performance characteristics available through component shopping. Consumers have a choice in the amount of memory desired, the number and type of disk drives, the level of sophistication in monitors and graphics cards, and the purchase of peripherals. Moreover, the emerging multimedia potential to be discussed in Chapter 12 requires additional technology such as videodisc or CD-ROM equipment. Yet, as noted above, many salespeople cannot explain the educational strengths of their various products to families, thus making it difficult for families to buy hardware and at reasonable prices (Wald, 1991).

THE INFLUENCE OF
PHYSICAL SURROUNDINGS

Human engineering, or ergonomics, is an important consideration in planning computer work environments.[6] While research on the designs of computer workspaces has focused primarily on employees in the workplace, little attention has been given to the location and design of computer space in the home, particularly in relation to children's needs. We identified several physical factors that dampened the use of educational software.

First, the lack of forethought and conscious decision making at the time of computer purchase led to makeshift computer workspaces and multi-use locations within homes. The decisions about computer location were usually made after the purchase, and often as a function of convenience or available space. Aesthetic considerations were more important than physical or psychosocial needs of family members. As a result, decisions about location rarely accounted for the users' physical needs or familial interactions. Parents, especially mothers, occasionally expressed more concern about a computer's appearance than about its uses with software. As one mother put it to a fieldworker: "This is a conventional house. There's no place to put a computer. Where do we put it? On the dining room table? That's where ours is. There's wires all over the place, hanging out the back. It doesn't look nice!"

More than half of the families chose to place the hardware in an individual's bedroom or study rather than in a common family area and paid little attention to the conditions of physical comfort, such as suitable furniture, space, lighting, or acoustics. One makeshift work station consisted of a computer sitting on a milk crate:

> The crate was filled with magazines and books and was placed at the end of the bed against the right side of the wall. The monitor was on one of the crates; the keyboard was on the other one; the disk drive was on the floor; and, the printer was on the pile of magazines.

Another makeshift solution "was a plastic case with wood flakeboard on it, in front of a small wooden chest. On top of the chest was a 13-inch color TV set connected to the computer. Charles [the son] sat on a wooden box in front of the computer."

In the majority of cases, the territoriality or ownership rights of a space often restricted other family members from using software. More than half of the families placed the computer in an individual's bedroom or study rather than in a common family area. In addition, as we note in Chapter 6, the computer location more often benefited the males in the family.[7]

The need for interaction in the use of software varied with children's ages, but was not addressed by many families. Younger children reported they were generally more comfortable being surrounded by other family members as they used the computer. For them, location in a basement den, for example, could prove to be too removed from the hub of family activity and opportunity for assistance.

THE CURRENT STATE OF EDUCATIONAL SOFTWARE

A perusal of existing software catalogues and of professional reviews of software makes clear the continuing mushrooming of educational software.[8] It also makes clear that since the mid-1980s many more potentially useful pieces of software and software systems have come on the market:

> The quality of software has improved significantly in the past three years. . . . [Therefore] computers can be excellent tutors for children at home, if they are used wisely. This means that software should be carefully evaluated and used to address skills that parents want their children to have. . . . But whatever the use, the interactive nature of the computer puts it far ahead of most other media as a means of helping young children develop cognitive skills critical to later learning. (Caldwell, 1986, p. 13)

Recently, Becker (1991, p. 7), perhaps the foremost researcher of the actual uses of computers in schools, has acknowledged educational software's increased quality and scope:

> Not only are there more topics "covered" by tutorial and drill software, but approaches to using computers have expanded to

incorporate elaborate simulations, games and puzzles requiring reasoning and information gathering, and a variety of subject-specific tools such as mathematical toolkits, outlining and other pre-writing activities, and microcomputer based science laboratories.

In addition, Becker (p. 8) notes the existence of such simulations as *Robot Odyssey* and mathematical tools such as the *Geometric Supposer.* He underscores the availability of software and systems of communication such as AT&T Learning Circles, the National Geographic Kids Network, and BreadNet, which allow for collaborative learning at a distance.

In a recent piece on software for *Education Week,* West (1992) also makes clear the current sentiments of evaluators that software has improved substantially. According to West, observers now say that "many of the . . . education-software programs available today are far superior to those early efforts" and quotes a long-time educational computer specialist as saying that "we can't blame the software any more, we have to take the responsibility for using it well or using it badly" (pp. 11–12).[9]

In summary, the argument over the quality and quantity of educational software has been about whether to "view the glass as half empty or half full." Critics rightly pointed out that much, maybe most, of the academic software in the early to middle 1980s was not superb. At the same time, there were many good programs that could have been useful had parents taken the time or interest to discover them or had developers and proponents been able or willing to inform schools, parents, and children more effectively about them. The absence of educational home computing certainly cannot be attributed to the inadequacies of software today, since sound software and compatible hardware are now more available.

Despite the existence of good software – perhaps still nowhere near the ideal amount or quality – it will not necessarily get to families and be utilized. Without the awareness and energies of parents, schools, children, and software developers, it is unlikely that much of the good software will be found, purchased, and used. Even the "good stuff" today cannot be used by children without a helping hand. Many of the issues we take up in the next four chapters are related to this central fact. Educational software will not set the educational process in motion either at home or at school simply by having children sit in front of machines, booting up software, and letting the technology "do its thing."

NOTES

1. Epstein (1985) reported that *over* 10,000 educational software programs or packages had been marketed by the middle of the 1980s. The Office of Technology Assessment (1988) identified three major sources of educational software: (1) commercially published, stand-alone products, (2) integrated learning systems, and (3) public domain and shareware programs. Most estimations of educational software during this period focused on the commercially produced, stand-alone category. Had the other two categories been included, the amount of educational software would have gone far beyond the estimates of the time.

2. Levin and Meister (1985, p. 10) also argued that it is "widely recognized that the software available for computer-assisted instruction is largely inappropriate and of low quality." Bork, as quoted in McKibbin (1986, p. 56), characterized existing educational software this way: "The software being used right now in the classroom – be it drill and practice or problem-solving – is like a two-page book."

3. Tucker ("From Drill Sergeant," 1985, p. 2) adopted the following definition of good software:
   programs that are not only free of operational bugs but are also pedagogically sound. Like good curricula and good teaching, good software enables students to accomplish an important instructional purpose and to do so in a way that engages their intellect and imagination. The best software helps students acquire a conceptual grasp of the material and, with it, an ability to pose and solve problems on their own in a particular domain. Moreover, it does these things in ways that cannot be done as well by other means.

4. If one adds to the body of educational software the "adult" tool software that could be used by children educationally – e.g.,

word processing, spreadsheet, graphics, and data base programs, then the number would top 300.

5. While Apple, the computer of choice in the majority of schools, dominated the educational market and had the most educational software written for it, the best software programs seemed to be available for other kinds of machines as well, including Commodore, IBM, and other MS-DOS machines.

6. We are indebted to Ellen Katz (1988) for her thoughts contained in a paper she prepared on the ergonomics of home efforts in our families for presentation at the American Educational Research Association meeting held in New Orleans. We draw on her thinking in this section.

7. One could argue that the favoring of "male spaces" actually "caused" female alienation and discouraged their use of the machines. Or it could be that since males in those families were the users, machine location in "male spaces" was a consequence of use and not a determinant. In most of these families the reality was probably varying mixes of both dynamics.

8. We examined a variety of sources including 1991–2 software catalogues such as those from Cambridge Development Laboratory, Children's Software, Educational Activities, Family Software Plus, FuturComp, Garlinghouse, MECC, Meizner, Mindscape, Orange Cherry, the Learning Company, Sunburst, and Tom Snyder Groupware. We also examined a variety of published evaluations including EPIE's 1991–2 review of about 4,000 entries and EPIE's review of integrated instructional systems such as Ideal Learning, PLATO, and WICAT. We also had access to a wide variety of articles written by veteran watchers of the educational software world.

9. This is not to say that there is a consensus on the current value of software. While the Office of Technology Assessment (OTA) reported that the technical quality of commercially published educational software was improving and that pieces of high-quality software were available for the home and school markets, they also found general agreement that "most educational software does not sufficiently exploit the capacity of the computer to enhance teaching and learning" (Sivin and Bialo, 1988). In addition, OTA found that important economic pressures militated against the development of innovative software. The OTA criticized the software industry for the lack of sophisticated programs, finding that only 7 percent of the educational software developed or demonstrated concepts and only 1 percent proposed and tested

hypotheses. The industry responded that it is far more difficult and expensive to develop software that promotes conceptual learning, critical thinking, and problem-solving skills than it is to produce word processing tools or drill-and-practice games packages (Shao, 1989). Pournelle, a strong champion of home educational computing, critiqued educational programs in game format as having limited value: "The very best [educational] computer games . . . still suffer from the generic problems of [all] computer games. . . . [They] seem to hold a player's attention for a maximum of two weeks . . . you won't learn all that much history and geography in two weeks" (1989, p. 69).

Chapter 5

The Importance of
Parental Encouragement and
Assistance

While parents frequently recognize the need for their children to be successful in school, they do not realize the critical role they play in their children's academic achievement. Parents often assume that the public school will take the place of the home in effecting their children's growth. (Snodgrass, 1991, p. 83)

The number of purchases of computers and software in the 1980s might suggest that parents were making an important contribution to their children's educational growth. Among the families we studied, however, these actions alone did not lead to academic computing or, for that matter, to other forms of educational computing. Such actions had to be coupled with other conditions, critical among them being parental encouragement and assistance.

In this chapter we focus on the different kinds of educational help that parents can give children at home. In our study, some parents offered help with academic computing occasionally, but most offered none at all. The exceptions we found demonstrate the positive effects encouragement and assistance had on children's computing efforts. We discuss the conditions – including parental unwillingness and lack of skill – that accounted for why parents did not help. At the end of the chapter, we speculate about the presence of these conditions within newer "generations" of computer families.

FORMS OF PARENTAL ENCOURAGEMENT
AND ASSISTANCE

From the literature on the involvement of parents in their children's educational development, we isolated six important kinds of involvement at home: provisioning, goal setting, praising, modeling, coaching, and scaffolding.[1]

Provisioning refers to behaviors that produce the material necessities of learning. For academic computing, parental provisioning would include ensuring an adequate computer, ancillary hardware, space and furniture, and appropriate software.

Goal setting has to do with the establishment of clear purposes. An illustration of parental goal setting would be the insistence that a child spend a certain amount of time each day or week on the computer in order to learn subjects such as reading, math, or science. The importance of praising is evident from the vast behavioral science literature emphasizing positive reinforcement in learning. Parental praising would be reflected in their positive verbal expressions about children's academic computing efforts.

Modeling refers to exemplary behavior. Parental modeling might occur when a parent uses a typing program to learn keyboarding and his or her children watch. Coaching refers to such activities as offering feedback and suggestions. This could happen when a parent helps a child do a programming exercise.

Scaffolding represents a kind of mental and behavioral "propping up" during a learner's efforts.[2] An illustration of parental scaffolding would be working with a child on the word processing of schoolwork until he or she becomes proficient in these activities on his or her own. As the child becomes more proficient, the parental "scaffold" is gradually withdrawn. Modeling, coaching, and scaffolding are fundamental to the current notion of cognitive apprenticeship (see, e.g., Collins, Brown, and Newman, 1989; Honebein, Chen, and Brescia, 1992).

THE MINIMAL INVOLVEMENT OF
PARENTS WITH
EDUCATIONAL COMPUTING

We have reported that most parents offered little or no encouragement or assistance when it came to academic or other
forms of educational computing. Now that we have elaborated
upon the types of parental involvement, we can discuss this
matter in more detail.

Let us start with what most parents did do in the way of help.
Like the four families portrayed in Chapter 3, parents did engage,
albeit in widely varying degrees, in provisioning. To one degree
or another, they purchased a computer (or computers), ancillary
hardware, and software. And, they allocated space for the computer, the adequacy of which varied considerably.

In most homes, parental involvement did not extend beyond
this provisioning. The majority seemed to think that their
provisioning actions were enough to expose their children to
"educational computing" at home. Often this was accompanied by the view that since the world was being computerized, it was "a good thing educationally for our children
to be exposed early on to computers." Many appeared to assume that home computers would somehow take their place,
as Snodgrass observed, "in effecting their children's educational growth." In an almost laissez faire way, some parents
reported that their children were doing less educational computing at home than they thought they would. Others observed that their children spent a lot of time playing computer
games.

Less common were parents such as the following father who
tried to help his son:

> I think he [the son] takes well to it. But I'm not that proficient in it.
> It's like the blind leading the blind. I'm trying to show him as
> much as I can, and I don't know that much about it. And he's not
> learning it in school yet. He's not getting any kind of extensive
> training and he's learning from someone who doesn't know that
> much himself.

Most parents, however, were like the Smiths, the Greens, and the Redds. They set few, if any, *educational* goals for children on the computer; they did little or no praising; they did not model, coach, or scaffold.[3]

NOTABLE EXCEPTIONS AND
THEIR EFFECTS

Although little goal setting, praising, modeling, coaching, or scaffolding was uncovered, this is not to say that these never occurred. The following section contains some notable exceptions of parental involvement and discusses the positive effects that such involvement can have on the home computing efforts of children.[4] Such parental involvement was more frequently associated with educational purposes other than academic activities.

WRITING AND WORD PROCESSING

Paul, a sixteen-year-old, had to write a term paper with footnotes and a bibliography. Gary, his father, urged him to use their Compaq computer and the word processing package, *Framework*. Through modeling and coaching, Gary helped his son use the software's note card function to create an outline, footnotes, and a list of references. Initially, Paul felt he was being "pushed" or "forced" into using his father's computer and program. And yet, by the end of the fieldwork, it worked out well. Ann, his mother, explained the effect of Gary's effort on Paul this way:

> After his first lesson, he [Paul] came up whistling and snapping his fingers. . . . Gary succeeded in helping him to word process. Boy was he [Paul] happy. Holding out his paper, Paul said happily: "It works!" He paused and then said with a smile: "It works well, very well, as you can see."

In another family, Katherine discussed her husband's computer coaching and modeling with their two children using the *Bank Street Writer* software:

65

Both [children] use [the computer] well and do editing with it, and the writing is a real educational process. It [the computer] turns a task into education. As my husband sits with them and makes corrections [on the computer], they learn writing much more than they would by typing or writing with pen and paper . . . and during the time that it takes, they share with their father and feel good about it.

THINKING SKILLS

Tim, the father in another family, brought home *The Factory*, a program for developing thinking skills, to use with his nine-year-old daughter, Jane. His involvement did not stop with provisioning. He coached his daughter, provided her with scaffolding, and praised her efforts. As the fieldworker noted:

One of the objectives [of this software requires] Jane to repli-cate a rather complicated figure by going through a series of logically organized steps. One of the steps called "rotate" asks her to select the correct angle of rotation (45, 90, 135). She needs help with this . . . and Tim instructs her. By moving her away from the computer, he demonstrates rotation by having his daughter turn her body around to the desired angle. . . . It's hard for her, but she stays with it and Tim coaches her a bit.

MATHEMATICS

A clear example of praising took place in an extended family household. Here, the father would encourage his five-year-old son, Paul, to use the math program *StickyBear Numbers* by booting up the software for him. The fieldworker recorded this observation: "Paul [used] . . . the program in front of the family who cheered wildly and applauded when the boy got the correct math answers. Throughout the course of the investiga-tion, family behaviors supported this and any computer use by the child."

In another family, Chris, age ten, described how her father coached her in learning about math fractions by using the computer and *Fraction Teacher*. Chris told the fieldworker: "I couldn't understand some part of my homework and my father was trying to explain it and I still couldn't understand it and then he went to the computer and showed me and then I understood it."

We present the most thorough example of parental help last. Here, Eleanor Lawrence clearly exhibited the various forms of parental help as she and her two daughters, eight-year-old Patricia and five-year-old Kate, used LOGO. It should be noted that this parent provisioned by first purchasing *Turtle Graphics*, which uses LOGO commands, and by eventually purchasing a LOGO program. During one home visit, the fieldworker observed some of Eleanor's coaching and scaffolding efforts:

> After Eleanor got *Turtle Graphics* set up, Patricia started. She knew to type in "pen down," but asked her mother why she had to do this. . . . Eleanor said, "If you don't type in 'pen down' it won't leave a trail." Patricia repeated, almost to herself: "It won't leave a trail." As Patricia created her graphics there was constant interaction with her mother, who knew which commands had to be entered and who could be called on in all cases of "error." This meant that when Patricia was stymied she had an immediate resource. . . . I don't know if Eleanor usually hangs around . . . but Patricia was relying on her to answer certain questions. Patricia seemed content knowing the correct spellings of the commands and got a lot of satisfaction out of seeing her commands entered on the screen.

The fieldworker also noticed that Eleanor kept notes on how to help her children with the computer:

> Eleanor has . . . made a written list of commands for her children to refer to while they are working. She helps to figure out what is wrong [e.g., when the machine beeps] with a program. She consults the manual and works with them. Eleanor doesn't tell them what to do, but does prod them along by asking them what they are doing.

At another time, the fieldworker noticed Eleanor's attempt to encourage her daughter:

> When Kate finished her program she ran it for us. Unfortunately, the text did not get entered and she was momentarily furious at her mother: "You told me I didn't have to put 'pen down.'" Eleanor answered calmly, "Well, we learned something didn't we?" But, Kate managed to correct her own error and then she ran "Hi Patricia" [for her sister].

During another field visit, Eleanor recounted an episode to the researcher that further reflected this mother's computer coaching:

> Today when I picked up the children at school, Patricia had done a program in LOGO. . . . So on the way home . . . I asked her: "How would you make a flower with the same number of petals just like that, only larger?". . . At first she didn't know whether to increase the directions about turning right. I tried not to out-and-out tell her, but to make her visualize it – if she said RT 40 or 50, it turns more. And then she realized the petals wouldn't be in the same place, that if you increase the angle, it's gonna make a different kind of flower. That's the kind of concept that LOGO is; even if it's a beginning stage, [it] lets children approach [certain ideas] much earlier than they would in books.

The above recounting prompted the fieldworker to enter this analytic note about Eleanor's involvement:

> The type of dialogue which Eleanor carries out with her kids seems essential to their learning from what they're doing. In fact, if the parents don't do it, I wonder how much is actually learned from LOGO or any other program. Eleanor is a former math teacher and therefore takes an interest in what is going on and she is also equipped to enhance her kids' learning by drawing them out and asking them to reflect on what they are doing in school. She also makes a point of understanding the curriculum and investigating the mode of instruction. As she said, "I talked to the computer teacher a little last night at the PTA and I've concluded that there's not enough individual

attention, so I might be willing to have something available here [at home]. How much time they devote would be up to them. There are so many activities they do that there's competition for time, but I think they would enjoy trying out at home what they begin at school." At Christmas time the mother bought a LOGO program and an improved monitor so that the children could learn LOGO at home as well.

Eleanor's involvement with Patricia and Kate provides a rich example – though not of academic computing, as in the Quarles family – of how parents could be involved in their children's educational use of home computers. Eleanor did it all: provisioning, goal setting, reinforcing, and especially modeling, coaching, and scaffolding. The end result in this case and the others was greater and more effective use of home computers for education by children. These instances were, however, few in number, with most appearing to be temporary, sporadic, or lacking in intensity.

REASONS FOR THE LACK OF PARENTAL ENCOURAGEMENT AND ASSISTANCE

There were two central reasons why most parents did not get involved. Unlike the Quarles and Lawrence mothers, they lacked the willingness or the necessary skills to do so. Without the motivation, many parents did not provision, praise, or set goals. And, without the knowledge and skill, many parents could not model, coach, or scaffold. Moreover, because they were unwilling, parents did not make an effort to become knowledgeable and skilled. Conversely, the lack of computer knowledge and skill contributed to parental unwillingness. As one parent confided:

If I had it to do over again, I would not have purchased the [computer] until I could have afforded the complete set of software and the instructions necessary to implement it. You cannot appreciate how foolish you feel not being able to get things to work in front of your children.

CONDITIONS BEHIND PARENTAL
UNWILLINGNESS OR LACK OF ABILITY

A dislike of computers and lack of time were among the factors affecting parental willingness and skill. As we shall see in Chapter 6, parents, especially mothers, expressed an aversion to computers or little desire to use them. In particular, working mothers indicated that they did not have the time even if they had the interest. Some parents who did possess sufficient computer skills said that they lacked the time to find appropriate software and then to learn how to use it in order to help their children. Some parents, fathers more frequently, were not home in the late afternoons or evenings often enough or at the right time to work with their children. For some parents, expressions of "no time" or "too busy to learn" appeared to reflect an underlying unwillingness to give *priority* to this kind of activity in their lives.

Minimal attraction to the computer and lack of time were part of the complex set of forces we uncovered. As the excerpts below show, the lack of parental involvement stemmed from other sources as well. Many had different computing goals for their children, such as computer literacy, programming, and word processing. Others deferred to their children's lack of interest. Still others believed that the school should set their children's computer agenda and teach them accordingly. And, as we saw in Chapter 4 and will touch upon again here, many parents believed that their children did not need to engage in academic computing at home, or felt that educational software was too costly, especially in view of its "poor instructional value," according to some. Irrespective of cost, some also believed educational software to be ineffective. Figure 5.1 contains a model that summarizes how these multiple forces impinged on parent encouragement and assistance.

When asked what kinds of families most legitimately would use computers for education, Timothy, a major computer user himself and the father of an eleven-year-old daughter, countered: "Computers are not essential [for children]. What's needed is more math and science – no frills.

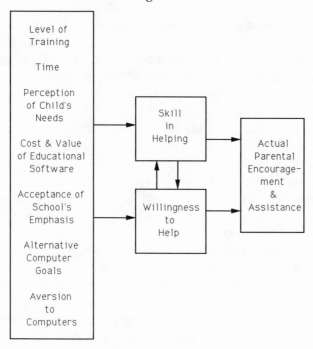

Figure 5.1. Conditions related to parental encouragement of and assistance in their children's academic computing at home.

Some disabled might benefit but I am not convinced." The mother, Lucy, stressed her preference for programming and the role she felt the school would play in her daughter's learning of it. She also acknowledged her dislike of computers to the fieldworker even though once for about six months she had sold them:

> [Lucy] feels that it is important for her daughter to learn programming. The use of educational software she thinks is "more of a game than a tool for learning." . . . Programming is valued by both parents. . . . They report that the difficulty the father has about teaching Joanna [the daughter] has also prevented him from teaching his daughter programming. The parents feel that Joanna will learn programming in her school next year. Lucy describes herself as having "an arty nature that turns me away from machines."

Jin Ho was also a regular user and the father of a seven-year-old daughter and five-year-old son. He maintained that his children did not need the computer and that the school should determine his children's use: "The IBM PC is not easy to use by themselves. I run program for them. I don't feel the need of computer for them. The computer may hurt their eyesight." About time, he said: "I may be busy working on my own stuff [at the computer]. They should play more at children's level. . . . If they don't use [computers] at school, I don't want to bother them with new technology."

The mother, Young Sook, noted her aversion to computers: "I don't use it [the computer] at all. . . . I don't like it. Before I do computer, I [must] read a book. . . . I have to know how to start and finish and how to [make] changes. . . . It is too hard. . . . It is better to write by hand."

In still another family, a different combination of reasons for lack of parental effort emerged. Jenny and Sidney were asked whether they would consider moving the computer from their room into the bedroom of their two daughters, nine and six years old. Their hesitancy was related to the importance they placed on the school's computer priorities, on whether their children showed an interest, on the belief that their children did not need it, and on their low opinion of educational software:

> Jenny said, "If they showed an interest in it." Sidney added, "That's a chicken or egg kind of thing." Jenny said, "Let's see what having a computer in the classroom will do (which she didn't seem to have much expectation about in the first place) and if Mary [their nine-year-old] wanted to take a computer workshop." Sidney replied, "Most of the stuff is games. I don't particularly see the use of that. A lot of the other stuff is remedial software for a child having a particular problem with math or spelling or something like that. Fortunately, my children are doing very well. So, there isn't a lot [of software] I could see giving them.

The analytic notes of fieldworkers revealed how still other combinations of these conditions affected parents' lack of computer involvement. After spending three months in the field with a family, one researcher stressed the parents' lack of skill and aversion to computers and their reliance on the school to determine their children's computing:

> Although both parents were involved in and concerned with other aspects of their children's education . . . and both perceived the computer as an education tool, they appeared to entrust the direction of their sons' home educational computing to the school. As parents, they neither encouraged nor discouraged their sons' educational use at home. Moreover, . . . the mother and father lacked the skills and the desire to learn the skills necessary to involve themselves in their children's educational computing activities. As far as educational use goes, this family will probably only use the computer for educational purposes when the boys' schooling involves it.

A second fieldworker highlighted parents' alternate computer goals and lack of knowledge about educational computing:

> They [the parents] believe it essential that their children attain a certain level of computer literacy and that they also develop programming skills. . . . According to John, programming would allow his children to become clear and logical thinkers as well. Susan believes that a PC is more educational than Atari and the children would at least learn to type. . . . The parents in this family know that something more about educational computing is out there, but they do not know how to get at it, or what to do with it.

And still a third fieldworker underscored parents' programming priority, their perceptions of the high cost and low value of educational software, and the negative reactions of their child to the use of educational software:

> As far as the parents [in this family] are concerned, programming is the heart of computer education. They are not impressed with educational software. . . . For what it does, Leonard feels it costs too much and Marilyn, who has seen some educational software, believes that it is more appropriate

73

for "rote learning" and believes it fails to provide the real responses and the dialogue a child needs in order to learn. Craig [their fifteen-year-old son] also expressed strong opinions about programming versus software. He feels that there is no point in a computer program for subjects that can be taught just as effectively by a book.

THE CURRENT NEED FOR AND
LEVEL OF PARENTAL HELP

While parental help was not the only factor that influenced children's academic computing efforts at home, it was central. How likely is it, therefore, that parental help is now more prevalent or likely to become so? Part of the answer lies in whether the above conditions and beliefs continue to prevail in families with school-aged children and home computers. Another part of the answer rests with today's educational software and computers. Do they still require parents to give help to their children?

CONTINUED NEED FOR
PARENTAL ASSISTANCE

Much of the software being sold today (Ortiz, 1992; West, 1992) existed at the time of the study. This includes current best sellers, such as *Where in the World Is Carmen Sandiego?* (Broderbund) and *Rocky's Boots* (The Learning Company). In addition, now that computers have far more capacity than they had just five or six years ago, software with even more ambitious educational goals is on the market or in the works. One new emphasis is on software for thinking skills and for tool usage. And, as we shall see in Chapter 12, there is also educational software being developed for multimedia technology (e.g., see Honebein, Chen, and Brescia, 1992; McMahon, Carr, and Fishman, 1992). Children's use of such software at home may in fact require *more* parental help than is necessary with the straight academic programs developed earlier.[5] Conservatively speaking, if children are to engage effectively in academic computing today, they probably need at least as much parental help as they did earlier on.

Are parents helping their children more today than they were five or six years ago? There is some evidence that little has changed in this regard. Mothers, most often the dominant parent in their children's education, do not appear to be any less busy, any more interested in learning to use computers, or any more skilled. If anything, the household burdens of mothers are increasing, especially for the growing numbers who hold full- or part-time jobs or who head single-parent households (Coleman, 1987; Olson, 1990). Fathers' work patterns, which kept them away from the house or away from offering much educational help, are also much the same. Nor does there appear to be any substantial change in the often-erroneous parental beliefs about the kinds of children who could benefit from the use of educational software at home or about the quality of educational software.

At the same time, some recent developments may be encouraging parents to help with children's home computing and perhaps with educational and academic computing as well. The increased computerization of many tasks on the job or at the office has exposed working mothers and fathers in unprecedented numbers to computers and their uses. As mothers and fathers are required to use computers at work, their fear of computers or hesitancy about using them most probably will diminish and their computer skills and familiarity with them will likely increase. Although this does not necessarily mean that they will know more about the educational uses of computers, their increased familiarity with computers could reduce the obstacles that deterred parents earlier.

Also, parents may feel better about the educational uses of computers at home if their children's exposure at school becomes more positive. Perhaps the greatest increases in parental help may come from exposure to various home–school computer projects, discussed in other chapters, that have been springing up across the nation. If more schools connect with homes over the use of home computers for school work and if these programs include quality training programs for parents, parental involvement in educational computing may well increase. This will not guarantee the success of such programs with even a majority of parents. Nevertheless, parents will be more likely to help at home. The above dynamics, however, will take time.

In conclusion, parental involvement in their children's educational computing at home appears to have changed very little since the time of our fieldwork. If this is true, then, parents in great numbers today are neither encouraging nor helping their children with academic or other kinds of educational computing at home. It is especially important to underscore the beliefs and actions of mothers because of their generally more intense relationship with their children and the impact this has on their children's growth and learning. The two most successful cases of educational computing in our study – that of the Quarles and Lawrence families – involved computer-literate mothers who took a paramount interest in their children's learning. When mothers shy away from the home computer as a learning device, it is quite possible that many of their children will remain unmotivated. Why were so many mothers distanced from their home computers? We explore this question more fully in the next chapter.

NOTES

1. Already very considerable and growing rapidly, the parent-involvement (PI) literature has been concerned with many topics: (1) the PI concept itself, (2) its prevalence and quality within families, (3) the effects of greater PI efforts at home – especially children's gains in achievement at school, and (4) the development of programs – through schools and other channels – that will help parents become involved more effectively in their children's education and development.

    Many aspects of this complex body of writing and research are discussed in a special section of a recent issue of *Phi Delta Kappan*

(January 1991). An excellent and brief review of PI issues can be found in *Education Week* (April 4, 1990), more specifically in a piece by Olson entitled, "Parents as Partners: Redefining the Social Contract between Families and Schools" (pp. 16–24) and another by Jennings entitled, "Studies Link Parental Involvement and Higher Student Achievement" (pp. 20–1). Still another useful and brief review of ongoing projects and findings appears in the special parent section of the *OERI Bulletin* (Fall 1991, pp. 4–6) from the Office of Educational Research and Instruction.

The research and writing of Epstein stands out in the PI literature. In a recent article, "Paths to Partnership: What We Can Learn from Federal, State, District, and School Initiatives" (1991), she argues that most schools recognize the importance of getting parents more involved, but few have a plan or engage in the practice. She (1989) also posits that six conditions in families, ordered to form the acronym TARGET (Task, Authority, Reward, Grouping, Evaluation, and Time), need to become the focus of attention if family influence on children's motivation to learn is to improve. She (1987) characterizes families that do particularly well as "school-like families" in that they reflect the same TARGET qualities as good schools. (In our study, two that stood out in this regard were the Quarles and the Lawrence families.) Epstein argues that such families "know how to help their children in schoolwork and take appropriate opportunities to do so" and "often have persistent and consistent academic schedules of learning for their children from infancy on, with books and colors, shapes and sizes, and music and art as part of their early 'school-like curricula.'" She (1987, p. 131) says that school-like families "create school-like tasks for their children and reward them for success, but also match tasks to the child's level of ability and involve the children in active learning and not passive learning."

Another key author in this literature is Rich. In her view, the educational role of parents is to foster a set of megaskills in children: "the values, the attitudes, and the behaviors that determine success in and out of school" (1988, p. xi). She offers parents hundreds of what she calls recipes – activities designed to promote these megaskills: confidence, motivation, effort, responsibility, initiative, perseverance, caring, teamwork, common sense, and problem solving. She is currently working with school systems, as is Epstein, to see how schools can help parents better foster such skills in their children.

In addition to the TARGET and MegaSkills approaches, another noteworthy effort is under way at Academic Development Institute, which has reached 16,000 parents in 200 diverse school settings. Their work is based on a concept developed by Walberg called "curriculum of the home," which depicts a cluster of parent–child behaviors "found to be common in families where children succeed in academic learning" (Redding, 1992, p. 4). These include informed parent–child conversations, discussion of leisure reading, joint TV watching, deferral of immediate gratification, expressions of affection, and interest in children's academic and personal growth.

One tentative conclusion is that programs to improve parental involvement are effective in raising children's achievement. Anne Henderson, an associate with the National Committee for Citizens in Education, maintains (in Jennings, 1990, p. 20) that her review of forty-nine studies, entitled "The Evidence Continues to Grow: Parent Involvement Improves Student Achievement," demonstrates the effectiveness of PI efforts on children's learning. At the same time, Sharon Kagan from Yale's Bush Center in Child Development and Social Policy laments in the same Jennings article (p. 21) that research on the topic has not been "sufficiently precise" and that what is needed is "a more robust research base." Moreover, in a recent review of the literature on involving parents in early intervention programs, White, Taylor, and Moss (1992, p. 91) maintain that "there is no convincing evidence that the ways in which parents have been involved in previous early intervention research studies result in more effective outcomes."

Another tentative conclusion from the PI literature is that parents in general want to become more involved but that they simply do not know how to do this effectively, *particularly as their children reach adolescence.* The belief, however, that parents want to become more involved does not go completely unchallenged. For example, Walde and Baker (1990, p. 322) argue that "*some* [their emphasis] parents care deeply about their children's education, but far too many parents – and not just disadvantaged ones – simply don't give a damn."

2. According to Resnick and Johnson (1988, p. 146), "scaffolded learning" expands the idea of apprenticeship from a psychological point of view: "This theory, drawing heavily on Vygotsky's . . . theory of learning, describes learning as a situation in which a skillful individual, usually an adult, provides the frame-

work (scaffolding) within which the less skillful person, usually a child, can perform parts of a total task." Furthermore, they note that the parts "make sense to the child through their embeddedness in a larger context; they contribute to a whole, even though the child cannot yet perform the whole" on his or her own. The child gradually acquires the skill to perform without assistance. According to French and others (1985, p. 9), Sachs "describes how parental talk scaffolds child play by enriching the child's ongoing actions and providing a more rational structure, a narrative thread, for the child's actions." For still other depictions, see Polin (1991) and Snyder and Palmer (1986).

3. We are grateful to Inez Wolins whose paper on SITE families was presented at the annual meeting of the American Educational Research Association held in New Orleans in April of 1988. We draw on her thinking in this section.

4. We do not want to give the impression that parental efforts to help children use the computer educationally *always* led to positive results and motivated children.

5. Given the various technological advances, the possibility of greater hardware and software transparency exists. However, we see little evidence that these advances have simplified or made the software and hardware for education more user friendly. The costs of the hardware, nevertheless, have come down sharply.

Chapter 6

The Role of Gender in Home Computer Use

The computer is not as important an issue as some have made it, but rather another appliance which has many uses and makes life easier. . . . You can't fall in love with your washing machine *or* your computer! If they're interested fine, but to me it's not a big deal. (A SITE mother)

Much research on schools has addressed itself to differences between the sexes in their computer use and attitudes.[1] Although the importance of the *family* context for "the learning and enacting of gender roles" (Lipman-Blumen, 1984) has been widely recognized, few studies have focused on the extent to which gender-related patterns influence computer activity at home. The integration of computer technology into family settings has the potential for either minimizing or maximizing gender differences in educational and technological opportunities.

In this chapter, we explore similarities and differences in computer use between the male and female members of our study group. We give special attention to the responses of mothers. Six key findings emerged: (1) males and females differed markedly in type of computer use (fathers and sons showed a broader range of interest and usage); (2) females in the households used the home computers less often than the males, and mothers were particularly estranged from the machines; (3) males were the key agents of decision making about the home computers, and fathers were most often responsible for bringing the computer into the home; (4) the sexes held different perceptions and attitudes toward the home computer (their analogies indicated that the computer held a playful and recreational fascination for the males, whereas the females viewed it as strictly utilitarian, as a practical tool for getting things done); (5) interactions around the home computers often accentuated gender-role tensions between the parents and challenged the women's sense of competence within their homes; and (6) despite important generational differences, parental behavior and attitudes appeared to have a "gendering" impact on children's perceptions about computer technology.

TYPE AND AMOUNT OF USE

Males and females differed in the way they used computers. Males showed a broader use and interest than did females,which included game playing, programming, work- and school-related applications, telecommunications, pirating of software, and "tinkering" with the machine. Many fathers' occupations – as educators, programmers, salesmen, or technicians – seemingly supported their interest in the home computer.

Sons, like the fathers in these families, exhibited a range of computer interests, the primary use being game playing. Approximately half of the sons engaged in some programming and word processing; and a few were so involved with the home machine that they could be termed "hackers."

In contrast, daughters used the home computer primarily for game playing – often with their brothers – and for some word processing and graphics. Only in one family were the girls engaged in more than superficial programming. One daughter described typical interactions with the home computer:

> I spend about one to one and a half hours after school playing games, or if I have a difficult assignment I use the time for schoolwork. On Saturday or Sunday, I would say no more than two hours each day . . . I find that the games don't hold my interest for much longer than that.

For mothers, the primary and almost exclusive application of the computers was word processing. They did not engage in programming, tinkering, pirating, or game playing. While game playing was a major activity, mothers were definitely not partakers. Although several had tried their hand at games, they had eventually lost interest. A few others reported seeing some benefit in the game playing for their children. For the most part, however, mothers expressed their lack of interest – even disdain – for game playing:

> My son is always playing games on it. I've never played a game on it since we got it. . . . I never seem to feel that I have time for those kinds of activities, and really, I'm just not that interested.

> I hate games . . . I'm not even neutral about it. I hate to see people just sitting, staring at that screen, pushing little buttons. It'll turn their brains to noodles.

Mothers were particularly critical of the perceived violence in the game software. Even in homes where the computer was well-integrated and used by both the male and female family members, mothers spoke out against game playing. Only one reported she enjoyed playing games; however, she discriminated among various types, saying, "I could spend hours [at the detective and adventure games] but I don't like the shooting games."

A clear difference between the sexes was also observed in the amount of time spent with home computer use. Female household members used the computer less often than the males. Mothers in particular were estranged from the machine.

Adult female members of the households, including mothers, step-mothers, grandmothers, and in one case a housekeeper, were rarely major computer users. In fact, as we saw in Chapter 3, only six mothers could be considered major users. In sharp contrast, fathers were major users in twenty-eight families. Only nine of the daughters were major computer users, whereas almost half of the sons were major users.

The majority of the adult females did not use the home computer at all. One woman, a high school English teacher, who saw no need for computers in her teaching and was not knowledgeable about word processing and outlining software, asserted: "I don't want to learn to use them. . . . Human contact is more important!" Still other quotations from women echoed this nonuse:

> I never use the computer and don't intend to.

> I don't know anything about it and no one ever asks me to touch it.

> The only thing I know about computers is the way they look.

A pattern of generational difference, however, emerged between mothers and daughters. Although daughters were not often major users, they clearly had more interaction with the home computers than their mothers.

DECISION MAKING

Males were the key agents of decision making about the home computers. In the majority of families, the father was identified as the key person responsible for the home computer's purchase or adoption. In many families, wives were not even consulted about the computer purchase or arrival. In fact, even in one family where the woman was classified as a major user, she had not been considered when the decision to buy the computer was made. Another wife reported she had no idea why the home computer was purchased or even where it was being kept.

In many instances, women either deferred to their husbands or found their various objections and concerns overridden by their husbands' decisions:

> It was a little upsetting to me at the time Michael bought it because we really didn't have money to spend on a computer. I didn't see the use of it. I still don't . . . for myself. . . . Now he's talking about getting Justin his own computer and he knows I'm not for that.

> It was his idea, and he went out by himself and bought it at some warehouse. I was against it because of the money, but he was convinced it was a thing of the future.

Other computer-related decisions about location and priority of use also reflected male interest and need much more often than female. For over half of the families, the computer's location made it primarily accessible to the father or to a son. In one household, when the father was asked how the computer came to be located in the master bedroom by his side of the bed, he replied: "That was easy. I paid for it; I bought it . . . I'm the father and I make the rules around here." His wife reflected on her computer avoidance: "Let's not kid ourselves. My husband is really master of that machine . . . maybe that has something to do with my avoidance of that machine."

One wife complained about the computer location, saying that she would use it more often if it weren't in her husband's study. In yet another family, computer access for the mother and daughter was limited by the perception that the computer was primarily a tool to promote the son's learning. His mother commented: "You know that we put it in your bedroom because we feel you need to use it the most. . . . I use it very little at this time partly due to lack of time and limited interest but mostly because of its location."

Other decisions about the family computer supported the use by sons over that of daughters. One sister, who never had any difficulties related to school, was penalized because, as she put it, my brother "has gotten behind on some school projects and until he catches up, I can't use the computer."

Fathers' decisions and influences on computer use patterns were apparent in other families. In several homes the computer was "off limits" to other family members once the father came home and needed to use it. A daughter reported that she would have used the computer more often for homework, except that she and her father both needed to use it at the same time. In order to have some access, she would sometimes get a friend to call her father on the telephone, and when he left the room, she would slip in her diskette and begin to work. In another home, where the father originally bought the computer but then became disillusioned, the machine remained in its box during the course of the study. The researcher observed:

"The father seems to be the leader in this family and if he says no, it doesn't happen."

Researchers have concluded that various processes associated with computer technology have reinforced existing gender and power inequities (Sutton, 1991). Kreinberg and Stage (1983) asserted that "the most important task ahead is involving women in technological decision-making." However, our study suggests that often the females were not involved in the many decisions about the adoption and use of the home computers.[2]

ATTITUDES AND ANALOGIES

Males and females differed in their perceptions of and attitudes toward computers. In contrast to the females in this study, males frequently articulated their enthusiasm, appreciation, and special relationships with the home computer, calling it "smashing," "beautiful," "sexy," "my baby," "my mistress," and a "good friend." One son described the computer as an aid to relaxation, and another son called it "my good luck charm!" One father described his son's computer attachment: "He loves that thing. God bless him!" Another father observed his son:

> I would say he almost loves it; he's constant at it. I mean, he's home from school, his coat goes here, books there, runs into the kitchen, makes a sandwich and a glass of milk, and he's off to the computer. If he's there an hour, he's there six hours a day, and he's up to 1 or 2 o'clock in the morning.

Such computer involvement illustrates the potential for isolation from social contact that Turkle (1984) described as characteristic of computer hackers. For many sons, however, the computer provided social contact and approval through game playing and pirating of software with peers. As one parent said about his son: "He likes to get together with his friends and copy games and trade." Another father expressed the positive social connection provided through their computer use this way: "The computer is like a religion – when you have one, you want all your friends and people you know to get the same kind, so that you can exchange and trade software."

Many males seemed eager to share their computer expertise with others and became enthusiastic about teaching theoretical and technical aspects of computing. In contrast, the social component of computers for females was characterized chiefly by their dependence on other family members for technical assistance. The women did not share their computer experiences with friends. For daughters, also, peer involvement around computers seemed minimal. One daughter remarked that when with her friends, "We don't talk about them [computers] much." Another daughter, a teenager, said none of her girlfriends had computers, whereas some of her boyfriends did. She added, "I know a lot of boys that are interested in programming. Do you know a lot of girls that are?" A third daughter described activities which she and her friends preferred:

> Some of my friends have computers at home so it's not new to them. Only if the weather is bad do we use the computer. [Instead] we like to go out and go shopping or to the bookstores; sometimes we go to the "Y" or just hang out.

Many females saw the computer as decidedly asocial and labeled it "mechanical," "analytical," and "impersonal." One mother described herself as having an "arty nature that turns me away from machines and back to pens, paper, lines, and circles."

In *The Second Self*, Turkle (1984) explored aspects of the computer as an "evocative object." In our study, a clear gender difference emerged in the ways that men and women expressed their computer experiences and meanings for them. Their differing analogies suggested that the computer had a playful or recreational quality for the males, whereas it was primarily utilitarian for the females.

Repeatedly, the home computer was referred to as a "toy" for the males and something to experiment with:

> This is my greatest toy. Of all the toys I've ever had in my entire life, this is the best. I've had so much fun with this thing.

> Mom and I laugh at Dad. He'll go for days trying to figure things out instead of looking in the manual. . . . He does things that are not necessary, but "make him feel good" and in the long run it saves a little time and he enjoys it even more.

One father described his exploratory approach:

> I feel guilty playing with the computer three-fourths of the day, but it's always satisfying trying to find that ultimate capability. . . . The only way you can really know is to burden it, crash it, and when that happens you have to dump the program, reboot and start all over again.

On the other hand, women typically referred to the computer as an appliance or tool that either had or did not have practical applications for them:

> I like to use machines or appliances if they have a practical use. They make my life easier, and they free me from time-consuming tasks. The microwave is great because it saves so much time. But the computer doesn't do that for me. It doesn't have any practical use in the house.

> I didn't want anything to do with it . . . but in terms of the word processing function, I decided that it was important for work. . . . I need the computer. . . [but it is] just a labor-saving device, like a dishwasher.

> The computer is like a book or a pencil; it is a tool, a part of learning.

One woman observed that she did not know any women who hack around or learn more than they need to know on the computer:

> I think that men and women use and react to computers very differently. . . . Men spend a lot of time playing with the com-

puter. Women don't see machines as toys and pleasure, as recreation. Women see tools and machines as purely functional.

Although feminists concerned about inequalities in computer use have suggested that women might benefit from viewing the computer as "just another appliance" (Van Gelder, 1985), it appears that for women in our study the perception of the computer-as-appliance did not enhance their use of the machine. In a provocative observation about the importance of attitudes in the home, Hill (1985) commented:

> The question as to whether home computers are a boon or bane is largely a question of challenge and response. The answer will be negative if people relate to computers as extensions of technology and positive if they relate to computers as extensions of themselves.

We found a clear difference between the sexes in their personal relation to the home computers. One woman expressed the distinction this way: "David [husband] is enamored of it; . . . we [daughter and self] see it as utilitarian, like a vacuum cleaner. It makes life easier."

For the most part, the men and boys readily perceived an expressive potential of the computer and, in many instances, established a personal relationship with it. One father commented:

> The relationship that exists is much more emotional than I thought it would be. It truly is company. . . . It does its clicking and whirring like a dog scratching behind its ear with its hind leg. . . . It's like a dog you're trying to train. You find the right command and it will respond.

However, women overwhelmingly viewed the home computer as a technological tool with instrumental value at best.[3]

GENDER-ROLE DIFFERENCES

Directly related to the different analogies used for the computer is the fact that males and females differed in their perception of the subjective value of computer tasks. This difference between the sexes was related to gender roles within households. For many men, their computer was a necessity they could not do without. As one father noted, "I'd hate to be without one, that's for sure. I'd have a hard time taking care of it all without the computer."

In contrast, computer use for most women was clearly not a priority. Overwhelmingly, they spoke about lacking the interest, the need, and especially the time. One asserted: "As far as I'm concerned, laundry takes precedence over the machine." Other reflections were:

When I'm at home I have too many other things to do to be bothered. [My husband & son] play with it together; I do other things.

At 7:00 p.m., mother [referring to herself] finishes dinner, picks up dishes, does the floor, does a little ironing, and around 11 p.m. she goes to sleep to get up at 5 a.m. So tell me, when do I have time to go through computers and do anything?

One woman dismissed the recreational value of the computer for herself: "Since the computer is now a toy – a play tool – it's not anything I'm missing. Another said: "I don't have time, for one thing, and there are too many other things I like to do and want to do. I'd rather read a good book or visit with a friend."

Some had initially tried to find a practical application for the family computer but could not:

Some people get all excited about using the computer for recipes, but I think that's stupid, and I don't have the time.

Me, I love bookkeeping, and my husband said he would get me a special program for it – I tried it one time, but it took so much longer, it wasn't worth it, so I do it by hand, it's much faster.

I would have liked to have used the [home] computer for budgeting, but I just can't, the bills change too often, it wouldn't be worth all the adjusting.

One woman observed: "Most of the uses are things that men use it for. Most of the things women do in the home don't require a computer."

Clearly, for the majority of these women, the design, marketing, and interpretation of home computer hardware and software did not address their needs or the reality of their lives. As Gripshover (1984) has suggested, mothers view time in the home very differently from other family members, and they perceive the amount of time required to master computer activities as a burden rather than an escape or pastime.[4]

For many women in these families, the presence of a home computer highlighted the difference between men and women in household responsibility and time constraints:

> Daddy had more time than we did – Daddy comes home from work and he doesn't have anything else to do . . . he has time to spend on his little computer – like a baby.

> Gail said that although the housework is divided up 50–50, sometimes she feels like she is doing 90 percent.

Although daughters in this study were less articulate about their subjective perceptions and presumably did not experience the level of household responsibility of their mothers, it seems likely that messages about labor divisions in the homes were being transmitted, as noted by other researchers. In a study by the Math & Science Program at the Lawrence Hall of Science at the University of California, Berkeley, elementary and secondary students were asked to imagine how they would be using a computer at age thirty. Girls focused on the housework that a computer-robot would help them do, while the boys imagined using the computer for finances, data processing, or games (cited in Kreinberg and Stage, 1983). Kreinberg and Stage (1983) concluded that dramatic gender differences continue in career aspirations and attitudes toward household responsibilities and influence expectations for computer use.

MOTHERS' THREATENED SENSE OF COMPETENCE

For these families, interactions related to the home computer often accentuated gender-role differences between the parents, with a particularly threatening impact on the women's sense of competence within their households. The home computer became a source of friction between users and nonusers, often translating into negative feelings between the sexes. For example, when asked how she thought the computer had affected their family, one wife replied, "It gave us a new subject to fight about." She elaborated by saying her husband expected her to master the computer, finish the novel, and probably still do all her routine jobs.

In some cases, wives resented competing with the computer for their husbands' attention. One said she told her husband it's "either the computer or me." Other wives responded similarly:

> What I don't like is that what used to be "our time" is now your time with the computer chess program. You could play chess at another time – it didn't have to replace the time and the game we shared.

> There was a period . . . and still is from time to time when I felt very resentful about the time he spends with the computer.

For many women, their responses suggested they had maintained a "defiant distance" from the home computers:

> I don't want a goddam thing to do with the computer. . . . I don't even know how to turn it on!

> Make sure you include in your research that mother knows absolutely nothing about that machine . . . unless I absolutely have to learn it, I don't want to know how to use it.

Different from other family members, mothers for the most part expressed fear and low self-efficacy in relation to the computer as a machine:

I feel so tense when I sit down at that damn machine. Who needs it. . . . I can live without computers.

When I look at it, I feel paralyzed. It's scary. . . . [The] computer makes me feel insecure. . . . I almost wish they weren't invented. . . . I was more secure before.

Several women attributed their fear of the home computer to past negative experiences or a lack of experience with machines. One woman commented that her past history with machines and even kitchen devices was "not too good." She said that she was intimidated by mechanical things and has an impressive record when it comes to breaking machines. Another wife elaborated on her lack of past experience:

I guess I've always been a little dumb about machines. . . . I seem to think they will cause trouble. . . . I suppose it's because I'm just not used to machines. It seems to me that men are exposed to machines more right from the beginning so they feel more comfortable with them. Did you ever hear of a machine shop in your high school when you were going to school?

In another case, a woman whose husband was director of a computer laboratory and a professor of educational technology felt she had been left behind professionally because she was not a computer user. She and many other women attributed their failure to use computers to an inability to learn something new:

I am afraid of me – to learn something again. . . . I told him that I would never be able to use a computer. I told him that I would be dead before I could learn to use one. I would like to learn but I don't think it is possible, it is too late for me. . . . I let my kids solve it for me. I'm not good at learning new things, it takes me a very long time to catch on.

Expressions of fear were not typical of other family members; only one father reluctantly admitted his "intimidation" yet fascination for the computer's capabilities, while another father was "scared of a loss of control" that the computer represented for him.

Not surprisingly, for many women, the presence of the home computer raised issues and conflicts around dependency. They felt they could not learn to use the computer without assistance from another family member:

> With the coming of the computer, I have become dependent on my son. . . . It would probably take a long time for me to be able to use it without John's help.

> I need somebody in the house to tell me what to do in case I have a problem. . . . If I had a few instructions I'd be able to put it together but I just don't remember all those silly little things, the carriage, the this, the that.

One woman said that although she had been very afraid of computers in college, she would love to learn if she had someone to come to the home, take her by the hand, sit with her, and teach her. Yet another woman believed that in order to learn to use the computer for writing, she would "need to be spoon-fed" and was not convinced that her husband was willing to do that for her.

With the recognition of a need to depend on family members for assistance, some women felt chagrin or displeasure: "I don't like anyone having to extricate me when I don't know how to do something fancy at the machine." One wife expressed her conflicting feelings in the following two excerpts:

> I'll tell you something else that helped (gesturing to husband) – having my own private tutor. That made a real difference. I don't know how I would have done it on my own.

> I don't know what I did, but I wiped out the whole thing. My husband was mad at me and said, "Why didn't you ask me?" I said because I'm tired of asking you. I wanted to do it myself. . . . I sure did it!

Unfortunately for many women, their husbands' patterns of behavior reinforced an uncomfortable dependency. One husband was asked by the fieldworker why he was the only family member using the newer computer. He responded: "I haven't taught them yet. . . . They're more comfortable with the old one and call for help when they get stuck." His wife complained that her husband made her feel like a child when she went to him for directions. A fieldworker paraphrased another woman's situation:

> Whenever she does sit down at the machine and tries to become more proficient with the word processor, it seems as though her husband always comes in and starts pointing out errors on the screen. She . . . gets very flustered and embarrassed . . . [and] becomes so tied up with the embarrassment that she has difficulty making the correction properly and usually abandons the machine. . . . While she would really like to know how to work it better, she loses interest in her husband's presence.

While many women found the computer to be a new area of dependency, one woman did proclaim that it gave her "a sense of independence" because with word processing she relied "less on her husband for editing." In a family where the parents were recently divorced, the woman took pride in her newly acquired independence with her computer: "I was going to have a computer and master this little task. . . . I didn't need to do it like him, I didn't need to be like Stan. . . . It was my way of saying that I could do it my way, and that is all right."

The picture that emerged from these data was that most women were resentful, estranged, and primarily fearful in relation to home computer technology. Hunt (1985, p. 20) observed that fear is not uncommon as an initial reaction to computers: "Often this is merely a mild anxiety about trying something new." There is reason to suspect however, that the fear of technology expressed by many of these women was deep-seated and debilitating. Dworkin (1976) and others have suggested that the socialization through which women learn fear is a function of the female sex role. Borisoff and Merrill (1985) observe that fear of trying something new may also encapsulate fear of the challenge to sex-role identity that is implied in new behaviors.

Interestingly, the women in our study did not talk often about concerns for the computer's impact on privacy, health, or social connectedness. Primarily, their fear was related to learning something that they felt other family members knew but that they themselves would have great difficulty learning. One mother described her ambivalent feelings:

> When they're doing programming, I'm cooking, and doing the laundry, and cleaning the house. They're doing all the programming and I feel left out. But really it's o.k. with me because I love it that they all do it together.

Later, however, she said: "I had that terrible feeling I was going to be left behind. It was like having a conversation in my [family] home when my brothers would talk, my father would talk, but my mother didn't understand science so she couldn't."

Bandura (1977) has argued that such self-efficacy expectations greatly influence one's willingness to engage in a task and the effort and persistence one maintains in the process. The consequences for these women of fear and low self-efficacy in relation to technology may be far-reaching.[5]

IMPACT ON CHILDREN

Despite important generational differences, there was evidence that parental gender-typic behaviors and attitudes had an impact on children's perceptions and expectations of computer use. As described, the dominant patterns of household responsibility, decision making, and communication between the parents reinforced role stereotypes and positional hierarchies. These prevailing family patterns reasserted themselves in the families' computer activities and may have been influential in socializing children toward or away from computer use.

In contrast to the respondents in other studies (Miura, 1984; Kreinberg and Stage, 1983), the women in our study generally perceived computer literacy as important for the future. Although many of them expressed limited interest in or doubts about learning to use the technology, they recognized its potential benefits and future relevance for their children, both sons and daughters. One woman elaborately anticipated her daughter's future computer use:

> It's going to be part of her life. . . . [She] has always been exposed to it – she'll use it to create. It will be an asset in future research skills but primarily it will function as an arts tool, and she'll use the computer instead of a typewriter for organizing material and presenting the final product.

Another mother, expressing the view that her children will need the computer because all of society is affected by it, said: "I want them there," adding, "I'm scared that I'm not 'there.'" Other mothers expressed similar sentiments: "I want my daughters to be ahead of the computer revolution that's already starting"; "we really don't use the computer – all this stuff is for you young folk"; "it's nice for the children, but it's of no practical use to me."

Another mother, a nonuser, said she couldn't understand why friends of hers had not purchased computers for their daughters. Mothers optimistically believed that "technophobia" would not be an issue for the children: "It's great that the kids won't have the fear"; "it's changing in my daughter's generation"; "you know the kids will be much smarter than we are – they will be high-tech."

With a few exceptions, however, mothers were not actively involved in supporting their children's computer interest, as highlighted in Chapter 5. They did not (in fact, could not) take the role of teacher in relation to their children's computer learning, unlike some fathers who played games with, assisted, or wrote computer programs for their children. When asked about computer use, one daughter responded: "not when Mommy's home. She says wait until Dad gets home." Another daughter reflected: "I feel I'm like my daddy cause he works with computers." A son, when asked what he had learned from his parents about computers responded, "Everything from Daddy. Nothing from Mommy."

In these families, fathers and sons exhibited similar patterns of computer attitudes and usage. In general, they showed broader interest in computers than the females and often experienced their computer interaction as a recreational pastime. Between mothers and daughters, there were some important generational differences; chief among them, daughters did not express the same fear or lack of confidence in their abilities with the computer. One mother commented on her daughter's computer use: "She's not afraid of it. She goes right to it on her own. She doesn't need any encouragement – maybe four days a week she'll just go and do it on her own."

Although daughters – like their mothers – often depended on other family members for assistance and permission to use home computers, most of them had other learning resources – through their friends or in school. One daughter who was very proficient with word processing said: "I learned from my friends and from my brother." She subsequently introduced the word processing software into her school, where they in turn "use it in teaching the course."

One daughter's expressed use of the computer seemed typical of the school-aged females. Her familiarity with computers came largely through exposure at school, where she used the computer in reading lab and "for making pictures with a turtle using *Math Logo*." When asked to name her favorite computer activity, she replied, "making really fancy pictures." On the home computer she averaged one and a half to two hours per week, "mostly for games." Although she had written a program in BASIC (with the aid of a workbook her father had bought) she found it "boring because there is too much typing."

Several researchers have focused on computer use by school-aged girls. Miura (1984) found that girls viewed computer skills as less relevant to their futures than boys did. In a review of related literature, Lockheed (1985) suggested that girls were more likely to use the computer as a general-purpose tool for writing, drawing, and data processing than for programming. Becker (1986), in a national survey of schools, found a rough parity between the sexes in overall computer use and in word processing. Yet, disproportionately greater use by boys occurred frequently. Collis (1985) reported that girls more than boys tended to hold a limited view of computer uses and a stereotyped image of computer users, seeing them as bright and studious but not personable.

Despite reported differences between the generations, the children were not immune to the gender-role patterns and expectations that many parents assumed toward the home computers. In one family, the fieldworker observed "the children are aware of computers and their impact on families. . . . They feel that the computer will be a part of education and . . . being successful in school, and that everyone will use it, except for women who work."

In a family where the mother was a major computer user, gender typing was particularly apparent. The woman, a high school English teacher, used the home computer daily for word processing both curricular materials and a novel for which she had completed over 300 pages. Despite the computer's impact on her life, she was regarded by her husband and son as not interested in the computer:

> She really shows no interest in it. I could teach her or at least my son could, because I have so little time. But she never asks to learn. She is really not very good with machines in the house. . . . Any idiot can learn to work a computer or any other machine. It doesn't take brains. But it does take some attention to details. I suppose my wife just doesn't pay attention.

> She doesn't really know much about how the computer works or why. She only pays attention to the parts of it that she wants to use. I'm not sure why. Maybe it's because my father is always saying how my mother screws things up, like the video recorder. I don't know why, but she always seems to make a mistake with that. She seems to forget some detail of how to work it. And then sometimes she can do it perfectly.

In another family, the father speculated on the ways his son and his daughter might use computers:

I feel my son may get involved in the "innards" one day. I know my daughter won't, but he might get into the hobby end of it, writing programs and doing computer stuff. My daughter uses the computer just like driving the car. It's there and that's it. Whereas he might get into it.

For many families, the issue of gender-role learning in relation to the computer technology remained an indirect and unexplored question. Parents did not often comment spontaneously on sex-role patterns. When queried about sex and gender differences, parents often seemed to accept traditional patterns while assuming that cultural changes would occur and eventually alter their children's experiences. For example, one father commented:

Generally, females tend to be intimidated by mechanical things. I think it's related to math anxiety and their having learned that it's not in their nature. I think [my wife] is too intimidated, like most women, to try new things, especially when it comes to mechanical things or trying to fix something. It's what they were taught; it's the way they were brought up.

Asked if it would be different for a daughter if he had one, he replied: "Absolutely! She would be starting on the computer just like [my son] did . . . at the age of two and would grow up with it as part of her life."

As for parental behavior in most homes, however, the "default position" seemed to be a stereotypic gender-based response to the computer without any conscious attempt to foster new patterns for children. Despite some differences between the generations in computer usage – especially between mothers and daughters as discussed – the impact of parental modeling was apparent.

This chapter identifies the confluence of forces that have kept many mothers away from their family's home computers. Moreover, since mothers play an especially central role in their children's day-to-day learning (Ballantine, 1989), and since parental expectancies have been found to contribute to children's interest in and use of computers (Collis, 1989; Miura, 1984), this chapter also helps clarify why most children in the study group did not make an effort to engage in educational computing at home.

NOTES

1. For a comprehensive review, see Sutton (1991). Also see Collis (1989), Hawkins (1987), Becker (1986), Hess and Miura (1985), and Lockheed (1985). Some applied researchers and educators have not only studied this issue in schools but have also attempted, through policy and teacher interventions, to provide equitable access to computers and computer instruction (Sanders and Stone, 1986).
2. In general, the decision-making and communication patterns related to computer adoption and use reflected other decision making occurring in the families studied. Giacquinta and Ely (1986) observed that the "use of the microcomputer seemed to be shaped by or reflective of the existing family structure."
3. Data from this study are supported by observations of other researchers. In a study of twelve families, Tinnell (1985) found that all the wives who used the home computer did so to meet specific needs but did not dabble with the machine. In their studies of school-aged children, Hess and Miura (1985) reported that girls who were positive about computers focused on what the computers could do, while boys were fascinated by the computer as a toy.
4. In her book, *Once Upon the Future,* Zimmerman (1987) describes the problematic relationship between many women and technology in American culture. She observes that household technologies have not changed the division of labor in the home and therefore have not made women's lives easier. Despite cultural beliefs to the contrary, recent studies indicate that mothers continue to have primary responsibility for household tasks.
5. Gerver and Lewis (1984, p. 7) have cautioned that if "women continue to exclude themselves or be excluded from learning how to make the new technologies respond to their own needs, they will experience still greater vulnerability; individuals or groups who do not come to terms with the new information technologies may in the end be mastered by the very forces they have tried to reject."

Chapter 7

School Use of Computers

The increasing prevalence of school and home computers suggests that, at the very least, there should be thoughtful consideration of the educational potential in using machines at home and school to improve students' skills. . . . Few school districts or teachers have begun to consider the potential for making use of the best available software by coordinating efforts between the school and the homes that have computers. (Epstein, 1985, p. 25)

In preceding chapters we have seen how the quality and availability of software, parental encouragement and assistance, and mothers' reactions to computers influenced children's computer use. We now take up the school use of computers and consider how it affected children's home academic computing and educational computing in general. Children's and parents' reports, as well as school visits by some fieldworkers, revealed that the schools emphasized computer literacy and programming. School computer use – at least for most of the children in our study – was not infused into traditional curriculum subjects nor were children exposed to subject-related academic computing in school. These school experiences had an important impact on what children did at home.

In this chapter we discuss school computer use, parental and child reactions to school use, the extent to which teachers communicated with parents about computers, and how these affected home educational computing. We argue that the school's emphasis on computers had an important impact on the home academic computing of the children in our study as well as on their home educational computing in general. Readers are urged to keep in mind the connection between what happens in school and at home and the discrepancy between most school uses of computers and the expectations for home computers.[1]

EDUCATIONAL COMPUTING AT SCHOOL

Most of the families in our study reported that children had some contact with computers in school. Some elementary schools introduced children to computers in the early grades, while others waited until the children were in the upper grades. Some offered after-school courses. The schools these children attended emphasized programming, and most did not connect the use of computers with academic work done in school or at home. Only a few children spoke about using word processing software in school. No child mentioned using a data base or spreadsheet in conjunction with other school subjects, although the computer teacher in one intermediate school covered the use of these applications in his course. There were occasional references to game playing in school.

The elementary schools usually presented the children with an introduction to computers – or computer literacy. Comments suggested that this introduction was very controlled and often consisted of exposure to computers with little actual computer use. One third-grader described her experience this way: "We go to the learning center and the teacher tells us about the buttons – you never play with them and you never put your fingers on the disk and you never do anything until she tells you."

Schools emphasized programming: Two-thirds of the families reported school exposure to programming, usually in BASIC or LOGO. At least five high school students studied Pascal in school, one student took it in summer school, and one planned to take it. A few high schools offered FORTRAN and COBOL, and one student reported studying both.

The fieldworker logs strongly suggest that elementary and junior high schools offering BASIC and/or LOGO presented an overview rather than an in-depth study of these languages.

One elementary school child stated that in BASIC class they learned "how to use the two commands – print the name, go to line – that's all." A seventh-grader reported, "I can print my name across the screen" and "the teacher gave me a program and I had to change it around." When asked for an example, he explained that the teacher might give him a program that prints even numbers from one to twenty and that he would have to change it to print odd numbers.

Some children who had developed an expertise in programming believed that their teachers were not knowledgeable enough or that their computer classes were too elementary. A high school senior declared, "Most of the [computer] teachers do not know what they are doing. The teacher goes to her course before she teaches it to us." However, a child in an intermediate school did report an exception: "Mr. A. is an expert. He always gives us answers about computers."

Instruction in LOGO programming can give children experience in problem solving and introduce them to geometry; it can help make abstract concepts concrete and give children opportunities to experiment and explore. Yet the evidence suggests that the schools offering instruction in LOGO did not give the children any real understanding of what they were doing or a chance to actively explore in a LOGO environment. One third-grader, for example, complained that there wasn't enough time in a period to explore after her teacher taught a lesson. A sixth-grader described his LOGO class: "Each student sits at a machine in our library and the teacher tells us what to do."

It was evident from children's reactions to LOGO that teachers did not take advantage of the educational potential of the language. Children tended to highlight the fact that they "drew pictures." The following comment of an upper elementary school child was typical: "I know a little LOGO. I can draw pictures."

It may be that the emphasis on programming helped to keep computer use separate from classroom activities. On the whole, teachers were not integrating computer use into the curriculum. A few children did report using computer-assisted-instruction (CAI) software for math or reading but this software seemed to be limited to computer lab drills on skills that were not necessarily connected to what was going on in the classroom. Only one family reported that its high school made SAT programs available to students.

Two of the children who did speak about subject-related computer programs presented examples of how computer use could be connected with the curriculum. When asked what types of programs she used in school, a fifth-grader responded:

> We use all sorts of games. For example, in one game we have to match up the capital cities with their states, like these places that I've never even heard of. And there's this other game that's kind of like Hangman where you pick the name of a state or something and there's this guy or monster, I don't even know what he is, well he walks and every time you get something wrong there is a cliff and he takes a step toward it and if you don't get them all right he falls, he kills himself. . . . In science we watch an episode every Friday and you have to locate where you are, you're lost at sea and you have to determine your geographic location so that the coast guard can come rescue you. . . . In math we just go back there and do problems.

The second child was an eighth-grade boy in a public intermediate school. When asked if he had ever used educational software in school, Charles answered:

> Yes, I used it in science last year. The teacher brought in a program where you can do a simulation of the dissection of a frog. . . . We had done an actual dissection of a real frog in class before this.
>
> In French class we used a tutorial to help you learn the language. It was really neat using it. They have them in French, Spanish, German, and Italian at school. . . . I liked using it. Besides the list of words to review and questions, it also had games in it with French words. It had a game called $25,000 Pyramid and a game of Hangman. It was fun to use.

The use of these programs by a few teachers might have set an example for others, yet neither Charles nor his computer teacher thought it was common for teachers in the school to have their students use educational software.

Charles's computer teacher suggested that teachers in that school, and probably elsewhere, were not integrating computers into classroom work for several reasons: it was difficult to get teachers to change what they were doing, computer teachers were busy, teachers did not have access to computer labs, and many teachers had been disappointed with the quality of early CAI software and did not realize that better software was now available. This intermediate school was a magnet school for computers, and yet the computer teacher felt that the program was not what it should have been, that it was difficult to order software, and that staff development was lacking.

Occasionally a child reported that computer teachers allowed them to play computer games. One fourth-grader declared that this was all they did. According to a sixth-grader, it was the children who persuaded the teacher to allow them to play games: "My teacher was kind of a pushover, so by the middle of the term everyone was into games instead of programming."

It appeared that children were sometimes allowed to play games that were not educational, or that teachers may have allowed children to use educational software without guiding their use. It is possible that sometimes teachers did not present instructional programs in an educational context, allowing children to use such programs aimlessly.[2]

Although it may have been difficult for teachers to combine programming with the curriculum and to find educational programs that corresponded with the subject matter being taught in the classroom, it should have been easier for them to connect the use of a word processor with school learning. However, only a handful of children spoke about using a word processor in school and only one of them, a ninth-grade girl, spoke of the school teaching her to use a word processor for ease of revision.

Word processing can be used to change one's process of writing but apparently schools were not emphasizing this.

Rather, the emphasis seemed to be on neatness. Typical of the comments relating word processing to neatness was that of an eighth-grader: "Teachers like students to do their homework on the computer because it presents a neater piece of work."

On the whole, school computer use in most of the SITE cases reflected the prevailing thinking of the period (Becker, 1985; Ferrell, 1987): Schools emphasized computer literacy and programming and used some drill and practice software. Although some of the schools did introduce children to LOGO, there was no evidence that teachers were aware of Papert's (1980) philosophy of teaching LOGO or that they tried to have children use LOGO in ways that would help them develop thinking skills.

PARENTAL REACTIONS TO SCHOOL USE

Knowing what parents thought about computer use in school further illuminates what schools (and families) were and were not doing with computers and why. Parental explanations for their satisfaction and dissatisfaction help to shed light on the impact of school use on home computing.

Over one-third of the parents expressed strong satisfaction with the way their children used computers in school, even though few seemed to have a clear idea of what the schools were doing or of what they thought the schools should be doing. Just as parents approved of home computer use because children were learning something about computers – because children were becoming computer literate – so did they approve of school computer use. Parents valued comfort with computers and emphasized the importance of knowing how to use computers *in the future* rather than how computers could be useful to their children *in the present*. Some did not seem to care what their children were doing with computers as long as they were doing something. Many, as reported in Chapter 5, also valued programming and were satisfied when the school taught programming.

A fifth of the parents were strongly dissatisfied with school computer programs, and some gave more than one reason for their discontent. One mother spoke of "lip service" on the part of the school and noted, "It's very nice to say we see the computer, but they're not using it." A father noted, "They never brought in experts to help plan a program." A few parents complained that their children either did not receive computer instruction in school or that they did not have enough time to use the school computers. Others were dissatisfied with particular aspects of the school program. Some disapproved of the quality of the software the schools used or were dissatisfied that their children were using school computers to play games. Some wanted the school to teach more programming while others wanted the school to do something other than programming. A handful thought their children had an aptitude for programming but were not getting the advanced programming classes they needed.

EFFORTS TO INVOLVE PARENTS

There was little evidence that schools tried to provide parents with information about educational uses of computers, or make recommendations about computers or software. A few schools did offer an introductory course for parents but these courses did not deal with the use of educational software or with how parents could help their children use computers for educational purposes.

There was also little evidence that teachers initiated contact with parents about computers. One exception was the teacher of a fifth-grade boy. The boy's parents reported that they had been thinking about buying a computer and that the teacher's suggestion gave them the impetus to do so. The teacher, however, gave them no help in deciding what to do with the computer.

Only one school allowed children to borrow computers. Oddly enough, in this case it was the father, a teacher, who became interested in computers when his children brought one home from their school and he subsequently bought one that was compatible with the computers in his school.

Although it is possible that teachers were not interested in communicating with parents at all, it is also quite probable that teachers did not know enough about computers themselves to either ask for or give advice. One father was amazed by what teachers did not know:

> This [school] librarian you wouldn't believe – she didn't know how to make it return. She didn't know how to store it on a disk. I said, "Here's a manual. Open the manual." Everything she wanted to know was on the first seven pages in that book. . . . I don't understand the terror of the teachers with the computers.

He believed the difficulty was partly the result of poor teacher training. Speaking about a meeting of school librarians that consisted of an hour's lecture on computers, he stated:

> You can't learn a computer that way. . . . They [computer companies] apparently don't understand the fears. They need to assuage the fears of the teachers. . . . I don't understand how Pet could've gone to sell them a computer, how shortsighted the Commodore people could have been to sell the computers and not come in to make sure that every teacher felt comfortable with the computer. Because it would have been good business. Because if every teacher had been comfortable with the computer, they would have said, "I want one in my room." So instead they sold three to four computers and that was the extent of their sale. If they had only followed up. When I go into the school and into the library, I see the computers gathering dust.

If schools were not taking the lead in fostering better parent–school relations where computers were concerned, neither were the parents. Most parents exhibited little or no interest in helping the school or in finding out from the school how their children could best use their home computers. When asked what his children were doing with computers in school, one father responded, "I have no idea." Very few parents reported consulting the school about computer purchase or considered buying a home computer that was compatible with the school's computers, and those parents who did ask the school to recommend hardware did not solicit information on software. Only a few parents, such as Mrs. Quarles, asked the school to recommend appropriate software or purchased a software package because their children were using it in school.[3]

It is significant that only a few parents criticized the school for not giving parents information about computers. A fieldworker found one mother who was quite vocal about this:

> Mrs. Reynolds said there is no orientation for the parents explaining the computer programs available for the children. She seemed annoyed at the school's expectation that "somehow parents should know" about computers. There aren't even any adult education programs available for handling the software or to instruct parents in how to help their children. Mrs. Reynolds continued, "I don't know and can't help my kid. The school offers nothing for me to help them. By the time I figure it out it will be too late. But my kids will know and will be able to help their children. . . . They don't expect the parents to know and we don't."

Other research has revealed that parents and teachers rarely work together to support computer activities at home, as explained further in Chapter 11.

THE IMPACT OF SCHOOL EMPHASIS ON HOME COMPUTING

Because schools were not integrating computers into the curriculum or using them for academic work, they were also not instructing parents in how to use computers at home for educational and school-related purposes. This lack of instruction served to reinforce further the reluctance of parents to have children use computers for academic work.

For the most part, parents and children separated home and school use of computers. Parents saw a separation: "Her school has had no influence on our use of the computer at home." Children saw a separation: When a fieldworker asked a twelve-year-old daughter whether there was a relationship between having a computer at home and using a computer at school, she replied, "They have nothing to do with each other. At school, we're just learning about computers and how they work." Her father agreed that there was no relationship, saying, "They are two separate computers." The fieldworker said of the father, "He feels that right now there is no partnership between education in schools and home computers." This father did feel that eventually children would be able to review on their home computers what they had learned in school.

Fieldworkers, too, noticed a separation. One of them noted that it was strange that "any references by anyone about the home computer and other computers [were] always separate, as if one has nothing to do with the other, never any apparent relationships drawn." Another noted, "I think Drew [sixth-grader] really separates computing from his other academic course work. He associates the computer with game playing and programming."

Computer use at home was viewed not only as being separate from schoolwork but as mutually exclusive from it. Children spoke of having too much schoolwork to do (which kept them from using the computer), of being forbidden by their parents to use the computer when they had homework, and of using the computer when they had finished doing homework. For example, a fifteen-year-old boy stated, "I go straight to the computer *after* I finish my homework" (our emphasis). In fact, some parents even made rules forbidding their children to use the computer before they had finished their homework. Such rules further emphasized the gap between computers and education.

A revealing comment was made by the father of a family that had two computers, an Apple and an IBM. Although the father maintained that computer use could be educational, the following statement indicated how he really felt: "As a matter of fact we leave the AT [clone] locked to ensure that the boys do not experiment with real information."

Teachers also saw the use of home computers and school-work as mutually exclusive. Children told fieldworkers that their teachers spoke about equity, saying that it wasn't fair for them to do their homework on a computer when other children couldn't. Other teachers considered it important to practice handwriting. A fifth-grade child said her teacher was worried about cheating; if children word processed their homework, he could not tell who had typed it or if they had used programs to correct spelling and grammar.

While there was little or no connection between academic schoolwork and home computing, there were connections in other areas. School emphasis on programming could be seen in the home computing of children. Often children who were introduced to programming in school also tried to program in various ways at home. In addition, many of the parents whose children were being introduced to computer programming in school stated that they believed their children would be prepared to work with computers in the future if they learned to program. Fathers spoke of programming as "the legitimate computer activity" and as "the real stuff"; what was important was going "back to the raw capability of the computer."

Rarely did a parent try to foster an interest in programming that had developed in school. As reported in Chapter 5, Mrs. Lawrence, the mother of two young daughters who worked with LOGO in school, was an exception. She considered purchasing the language, and ultimately did purchase it, so that her daughters could "fiddle around" and practice at home what they were learning in school: "What I wanted immediately was something where the kids could bring home their enthusiasm and carry something on at home." She did not, however, want her daughters to spend too much time at the computer. Her two young daughters experimented at home with LOGO commands they had learned in school. The fieldworker reported that both of them "were pooling the knowledge each had gained in school and from consulting the LOGO manual" and that one of the children "seemed to be trying to replicate the program of repeated circles from something she had done in school."

A great deal of the educational computing that did occur was influenced by school programming and writing assignments. Indeed, some parents and children expected that there would be less educational use at home when children did not have such assignments, and more when they did. For example, with respect to word processing, an eleven-year-old girl who liked to compose on the word processor did not use her computer over spring vacation "because I didn't have homework to do." With regard to programming, a fifth-grader stated that he would not use the home computer "unless I had to . . . do some computer work for school, then I would. Last year, when I was taking the computer course, I used it." His eighth-grade brother reported, "No, I don't work on it that much [at home] any more – just to play games with my friends. Next term I'll probably use it more 'cause I'll be using it at school." A fieldworker who visited another family wrote:

> Rebecca [a tenth-grader] responded by saying that she was using it less, but that this would soon be rectified because she had assignments for school. Sue [a seventh-grader] also indicated that she was using it less. "But," [her father said] "I think it depends to some extent on the amount of homework that requires a lot of writing. . . . For some unexplained reason, this year has not had the high volume of written assignments."

As one of the fieldworkers noted:

> There seems to be a direct relationship between what is being taught at school and what is going on in the home in terms of computer use. The more computer activity there is in the school environment, the more the computer is used at home by the two boys, or at least the older boy.

In a few rare instances we saw additional influences of the school on home computer use. For example, when asked if he had ever worked on an application at home that he had learned in school, an eighth-grade boy, who had learned about spreadsheets in a school computer class, said that he had tried to use a spreadsheet with his neighbor. It seems reasonable to assume that had children been afforded positive experiences with educational computer software in school – with academic and with tool programs – they would have been motivated to use such software at home and might have asked for it. Parents, in turn, would have been more likely to purchase such programs.

Where did the parents get their ideas – their interest in computer literacy and in programming? Were they influenced by the school's emphases or by the then current ideas about computers? Educator interest in computer literacy and in programming was widespread at that time. Although it is difficult to separate the influence of the school and that of the prevailing thinking at the time, our data reveal that schools either reinforced the beliefs and actions of the SITE families, which may have been influenced by the then current ideas about computers, or they shaped these beliefs. If schools had emphasized other educational uses, parents might have become aware of them, considered them important, and tried to foster their home use. Children, too, might have taken more of an interest in educational computing. In conclusion, how children and their parents viewed and used (or did not use) computers was in most families influenced strongly by what was or was not happening in their children's schools.

THE CURRENT STATE OF SCHOOL COMPUTING

When the SITE study began in 1984, some educators were already beginning to criticize the way computers were used in schools:

> Computers could do . . . better, say some educators, if they were used to their full potential. Rather than taking advantage of the computer's full interactive and graphics capacities, many schools only serve up repetitious drill-and-practice programs designed to supplement classroom instruction. They use the computer as an "electronic workbook." (Powell, 1984)

Educators also wanted children to use more open-ended software over which they had control. More of this type of criticism would come in later years.

By 1987, when the SITE study ended, many researchers who were interested in the educational use of computers had begun to shift their emphasis from computer literacy and programming to integrating computers into schoolwork and to using them with word processing, spreadsheet, and data base programs ("Educational Technology 1987," 1987; Ferrell, 1987; Sheingold, Martin, and Endreweit, 1987). Such activities would make computers an integral part of schoolwork and would be quite different from the occasional computer use that had taken place earlier.

Becker (1986, p. 10), for one, found that teachers "were coming to believe that the best way to use computers at their school was as a tool to help students accomplish concrete tasks – tasks in writing, problem solving, data analysis, and perhaps other areas." The interest in integration and in the tool use of computers was soon evident throughout the professional literature. Magazines for teachers, such as *Classroom Computer Learning* (now *Technology and Learning*) and *Teachers and Computers,* began to offer practical advice on how to coordinate computers with classroom studies. Newspaper articles, too, introduced the idea to the public (see, e.g., Fisher, 1988). Companies started producing software with the curriculum in mind (Brady, 1988; Shalvoy, 1987a).

Interest in programming declined as more and more emphasis was placed on coordinating computer use with classroom studies. This was especially true in the elementary schools. Also, educators began to suggest ways of connecting programming – especially LOGO programming – with the curriculum. At the LOGO 1986 conference, educators discussed linking LOGO programming with the curriculum, and *LogoWriter,* a new version of LOGO, "with its text features, and subject-related idea booklets, [was] a good example of this shift in emphasis" (Salpeter, 1986, p. 49). Rosen (1987) described how students can use *LogoWriter* to work on projects related to the curriculum.

Although some computer educators continue to believe in LOGO programming, using either LOGO software or *LogoWriter,* the teaching of LOGO, especially as advocated by

Papert, has not become a main focus for schools. It would be extremely difficult if not impossible for teachers or parents who are not computer experts or LOGO experts to provide children with adequate support as they experiment with the language.

Some educators are interested not only in tool use but also in integrated learning systems (ILSs). With an ILS, students can work individually to learn material and to practice skills related to the curriculum (Mageau, 1992).

Over the years, hardware and software have improved. Educators have advocated new uses for school computers that have been tried in some schools, and new educational applications continue to develop. One new trend is the use of telecommunications (Knapp, 1987; Shalvoy, 1987a; Reinhold, 1987). With a telephone line and a modem, students can access online information services, send and receive electronic mail, and engage in teleconferencing. Students can use online information services to conduct research and, with electronic mail and teleconferencing, they can also collaborate on projects with students from other schools in this country as well as abroad and with adults, too. These activities can be integrated into particular subject areas.[4]

In spite of the apparent interest in integrating computers into the curricula in these ways, and in spite of descriptions of how selected teachers have been using computers in their classrooms with excitement and success, few schools appear to have reached this point. The fact that there is much interest in these new educational uses of computers does not necessarily mean that they are actually taking place. The enthusiasm over the use of computers at school has been accompanied by an undercurrent of disappointment and realization that there is widespread resistance to computers, that integration is less than has been reported, and that integrating computers into the curriculum, even if only for occasional ancillary academic learning, is not an easy task (Ellison, 1989; Fisher, 1988; LaFrenz and Friedman, 1989; Levin, 1990; Winn and Coleman, 1989). If children were using school computers for educational purposes at school and enjoyed doing so, then they might be motivated to use the computer for similar purposes at home. We turn next to a discussion of children's interest in computers.

NOTES

1. We are writing with the knowledge that current promoters of educational computing recommend the integration of computer use into the curriculum. We recognize that the school use of computers is still in its infancy and that schools are groping about for the appropriate application of the new technologies.
2. It also seems likely that some children used the word "game" to describe any educational software they enjoyed, whether or not they were aware of its instructional purpose.
3. Mrs. Quarles, the mother who pressured her children to use educational software for reading and math, was one of the few parents who took the initiative to consult with teachers about appropriate software to use at home. When asked how she knew what her children were doing in school, she replied, "I know exactly what each of them is doing in school because I make it my business to know." Before purchasing software, she would speak with the children's classroom teachers and with the media teacher. As a parent who volunteered in the school, she was able to speak informally with teachers.

   Even parents who were knowledgeable about computers did not usually get involved with the school's use of computers. Being knowledgeable about computers does not necessarily mean being interested in or knowledgeable about the educational uses of computers. A father who worked for IBM did not want to get involved in what the school was doing with computers. Another father was interested in computer programming and served on the school computer committee but still did not know much about the school's use of computers. The fieldworker recounted, "I asked him if the school uses any academic microcomputing software in the math and science classes, or any other class, and he answered, 'I have no idea.'" Yet another father, who voiced interest in the school's use of computers, made a statement that seemed to sum up his true feelings. He related that the principal had asked the father of another child in the school to help the school choose software:

He's one of the top consultants in the field and it was just ridiculous to say to his boss "excuse me I have to leave at 3 p.m. to teach some kids." I guess only mothers volunteer, not fathers. They have to work and that's more important.

An exception was a father who tried to influence the school district's computer program by working with the district on computer planning. In addition, he had placed a computer in his younger child's nursery school and had made a presentation at his older daughter's elementary school on the use of computers in art.

4. Another current trend is an interest in multimedia, which we will discuss in Chapter 12. In addition to attempting to integrate computers into the curriculum, a few school systems have established programs that loan computers to children and their families. We will discuss some of these programs in Chapter 11.

Chapter 8

Children's Preference for Games

The key to using microcomputers . . . is to see the machine as a tool or toy that makes possible things that were formerly impossible. . . . The machine must be viewed as a toy in its best sense: namely, something that is non-threatening, enjoyable, entertaining, and that provides information or a service we find useful. (Silvern, 1987, p. 80)

As we have seen, the perceived quality and availability of educational software had an effect on home educational computing among the children in our study. The degree of parental leadership, the role of gender, and school emphasis also contributed to the lack of home effort. Children's strong preference for games was another important force that kept children from engaging in educational home computing and increased the likelihood of their lack of receptivity to such endeavors.

It is common knowledge that children (as well as adults) are intrigued by computer games. Educators have tried to analyze this fascination (Greenfield, 1984; Malone, 1984; Perkins, 1983) and journalists frequently write about the widespread interest in video games.[1]

In this chapter we compare the children's clear attraction to the playing of computer games to their rejection of academic computing. We discuss some of the reasons for these positive and negative reactions and examine how the conceptions parents and children had of computers may have affected reactions to computer games and to educational software.

THE PULL TOWARD GAMES

Game playing was the primary computer activity for most of the children in our study. Fieldworkers frequently observed that "the children spend as much time as they can playing with the games" and "they seem to gravitate toward games." This was true even though over half of the families stated that they purchased their home computer mainly or partly for educational purposes, and only four families reported that they purchased their computer primarily for recreation. Even when the reason for the purchase was said to be education, family behavior proved otherwise. A thirteen-year-old confessed that he had manipulated his parents into getting the computer: "Originally, I told my dad I needed a computer for school, but I really wanted it to play games." When a fieldworker asked a sixteen-year-old boy if he had bought the computer to help with schoolwork, he replied, "On pretense, of course!"

PEER AND SIBLING SUPPORT

Peers supported game playing and the copying of games. Using the computer was often a social occasion that revolved around games and frequently involved trading them. Even children who did not often use the computer sometimes played games with friends. As one fieldworker noted, "Melissa has used the machine only four or five times strictly for games and it's been when other people have come over – it's been a form of a social entertainment." Children who were more involved with gaming made statements such as, "I just use the computer to play games with my friends."

Along with friends, siblings also supported the use of the computer for games. One mother noted:

> It's funny. Stuart will either be on it quite a bit for several days or he won't be on it at all. I mean for fun and games he'll be on it. . . . He starts then usually his sister will do it. He'll say I found this in this dragon or something and then she'll want to get on it. Especially when they've solved something in one of those mystery things that they have. They'll be hooked on that for a

few days. Then if a friend comes over he'll do it with one of his friends.

PARENTAL SUPPORT

Parents, especially fathers, tended to accept game playing. Some actively supported it by buying games, getting copies of games for their children from friends, preparing a game disk for children to use, booting up games for their young children, and playing games both alone and with their children.

In some families, the playing of computer games provided an opportunity for social interaction between parents and children. A sixteen-year-old boy related:

> Sometimes my dad comes home from work and says, "Hey you want to play a game on the computer" – he loves this one game called "The Gambler" – so I guess, well, that takes about a half an hour. And well, my mom, well when my friends come over and we're playing a game or doing a program, she tries to watch what we're doing to learn about it and stuff.

A high school senior stated that he had borrowed a couple of games and that he knew that his father would want to play with them: "All I have to do is get the joysticks."

Several families owned chess programs and at least two fathers often played chess with the computer. *Flight Simulator* was another game with which fathers were intrigued. According to one wife, her husband had "wasted an entire weekend" playing it.[2]

A few parents did object to having their children play computer games or disapproved of the amount of time their children spent playing games. One was Mrs. Quarles, who favored her children's use of drill and practice software: "I feel that games take away from what the kids are supposed to be really doing when they are using the computer." In addition, others voiced a desire for their children to "graduate to the other uses of the computer," saying, for example, "I like them to do the games but I really wish they would want to do the educational ones a little more than they do." Although a few of these parents did forbid game playing, the main action they usually took – if they did anything at all – was to insist that homework be finished before their children used the computer. With rare exceptions, these parents did little or nothing to find out how their children might be making educational use of their computers and took no steps to lead their children toward other uses, thus supporting the playing of games if only by default.

REASONS PREFERRED

Some educators have concluded that children may learn specific skills from video games. Bowman (1982, p. 16) writes that "video gamesmanship represents conscious, deliberate mental and physical activity. It promotes active learning by shifting players into the participant role." Greenfield (1984, 1985) has given considerable thought to video games and thinks that by playing them people learn about the computer, develop eye–hand coordination, develop spatial skills, learn to deal with various types of complexity, and develop thinking skills that are important in the scientific process. "Video games are . . . an informal learning mechanism that helps to develop the scientific thinker who is able to approach complex systems with unknown rules and figure them out, just as a video player figures out the game" (Greenfield, 1985, p. 21).

Several of the children claimed that games taught them something and that games were educational as well as fun. A seventh-grade boy, speaking about the game *Eastern Front*, said, "It requires serious general strategy, a lot of thought. I think it's educational, not just practical." A fieldworker recorded the following conversation she had with another tenth-grade boy:

> He begins to explain to me that Zork is more than a game; it is an exercise in thinking analytically and logically. It also helps with his spelling because, he says, "I see words that I would not normally see or learn about in school."

A few parents expressed the opinion that children learned something by playing games and that game playing could teach children valuable skills, such as eye–hand coordination ("His hand–eye coordination has improved. It is "fan-tastic."):

You know all of them in different ways are of value in teaching him certain things. Like those adventure games and "Dungeons and Dragons," they taught him some discipline, they taught him how to spell, they taught him vocabulary. The experience of dealing with those things helped him to increase his attention span.

There is an educational throw-off incidental to some of the games. . . . I don't know if it's intended or not but a certain amount of the games require thinking, logical progression abilities, vocabulary, [and] concepts that children would not otherwise deal with.

In a few families, parents claimed that they tried to purchase games that fostered the development of thinking skills. One father, for example, said that he tried to purchase "games that encouraged intellectual reasoning and coordination." In another case, the fieldworker noted:

Phyllis [the mother] described the fact that the new games that Paul [the father] had bought were thinking games. You followed clues making choices to try to reach a goal. She felt that the kids were thinking more. . . . Paul added that Rebecca had become more analytical as a result of using the computer. . . . Phyllis felt that the new games were completely different because the user was actively engaged with the computer.

On the other hand, many of the parents thought that just by playing games their children were learning something about the computer and becoming comfortable with it. Parents made statements such as: "Even by playing games, you become very comfortable" and "Joysticking it – even for two or three years – will be helpful to them." Since the main reason that parents seemed to support computer use in general was to have their children become exposed to and comfortable with computers, any use would have appeared to serve this purpose.

Another consideration is that parents may have thought that they had no alternative. Whether they liked it or not, their children were going to use computers for playing games. Thus, their reasons for finding value in computer game playing may have been influenced by their need to justify it. If they could make themselves believe that game playing served a purpose, they would feel better about it.

THE PUSH AWAY FROM
EDUCATIONAL SOFTWARE

Ten to fifteen years ago, before home computers were as common as they are now, some researchers were reporting that children had positive attitudes toward computers and that they were motivated by school computer use (Clement, 1981). Such use was usually computer-based programmed instruction. However, others were beginning to speculate that children's increasing experience with home computers and with video games might have an important bearing on their conceptions of and expectations of computers. Becker (1982), for example, wondered if the similarity of school computers to video game machines would make them dislike educational use. Williams, Coulombe, and Lievrouw (1983) considered that the presence of home computers might affect children's attitudes toward educational computing. When we considered child receptivity to educational software, we found that most children were not motivated by educational software; the excitement of computer games may very well have affected their perception of the educational programs they used. As the mother of an eleven-year-old boy put it, although they had purchased the computer for educational purposes, "education soon paled and he plunged immediately into games with a passion."

LACK OF CHILD RECEPTIVITY

For the most part, children's experiences with academic software, at home and at school, were not positive during the time of our study. Some found software unexciting, a reaction that might be expected of children who were used to the stimulation of video games. Fieldworkers described the negative reactions of children to the educational software they had tried, reporting that children complained that school software was "dumb" and "boring" and that drills were "not challenging" and had "a lot of repetition." A fieldworker noted that when a fifth-grade child was asked about her math game, her "face scrunched up with dislike," and another fieldworker "noticed that all of the educational disks that [a child's] mother had purchased had been erased and games were placed on them instead." Andrew Quarles's mother required him to use academic software but this did not mean that he had to like it: "Using it for schoolwork bores me," he said. His dislike of educational software did not prevent him from liking computer games.

Sometimes when parents did purchase educational software, it was inappropriate to their children's ages or needs. At other times, children found it difficult to use the programs. Because children received little or no encouragement from parents, siblings, peers, or school to engage in educational computing, there was no social force to counteract their fascination with games and their negative experiences and lack of receptivity to educational computing. The pull toward game playing was reinforced by the push away from educational software, with the result that game playing was allowed to remain the dominant computer activity.

There is another factor to consider. It is possible that children may be more willing to use educational software at school than at home; after all, children usually expect to work in school but not at home, where there are other attractions, including that of computer games. A twelve-year-old girl who did not like educational software anyway stated her position bluntly: "I don't like learning on the computer; what do you think – I go to school and I'm going to come home and do more work. No way."

LACK OF PARENTAL RECEPTIVITY

As explained in Chapter 4, the parents in our study knew little about educational software and about the educational uses of computers. Many believed that educational software was not very good and that the educational application of computers was most beneficial to children who needed remedial help. Many seemed confused and ambivalent about educational programs, although some could give lip service to their value. All in all, though, parents were not receptive to educational software, knew that their children were not receptive to it, and made little or no attempt to find out about educational software or to encourage their children to use it. Lack of knowledge about educational software and lack of receptivity to it may have been important factors leading to parental acceptance of the use they did see: game playing.

THE POSITIVE INTEREST OF SOME CHILDREN

Although evidence indicated that most children were not receptive to educational software, there were exceptions. By looking at them, we can begin to understand the circumstances that might lead to more constructive computer use. In the following cases, children's receptivity to educational computing was linked to their conception of computers: They were beginning to understand that computers could make their schoolwork easier and more enjoyable.

When children did have positive feelings toward educational computing, they were more likely to favor the use of a word processor than the use of academic software. Several children claimed that using a word processor motivated them to write. A fifteen-year-old girl found that doing her writing assignments on the computer made it more "fun": "It's fast and it comes out so neat. I can make corrections without having to rewrite." A twelve-year-old boy had this to say: "Before I used the computer, I hated to write." He explained:

> Without being able to type my papers I don't think I'd write as much or do as well. I know the computer doesn't think for me, but it has made it easier for me to do my schoolwork. It's not so tedious using the machine as sitting at a desk doing something with a pencil and paper. I'm not sure why that's so. It just is. I don't mind doing my homework so much on the computer.

His mother was pleased:

I've seen what I think is great improvement in my son's writing since he has used the processor. Of course, he's also getting older and knows more every day, so I'm not positive it's the computer that has helped so much. Still, when he has to write things out with a pencil or pen, he groans and complains so. If it just does away with the groaning, it's worth it.

In a few families, siblings or peers supported the use of educational software, indicating that educational computer use can be social and that it can be fun. A high school junior enjoyed working with his friends on programming homework for computer class and also helped a friend who was not doing well in the course. The two young Lawrence sisters who used LOGO at home enjoyed using it together. The fieldworker noted:

> Their enjoyment was obvious; they were singing out the commands, whistling, clapping, laughing. At some point Patricia realized that she hadn't named the program and would therefore have to start all over again. Undaunted, they began again, this time reciting the commands in unison. . . . Kate was jubilant. She sang, "End, end, end, circle defined." Patricia read from the screen, "Saving it" and clapped and laughed as the circle was traced on the screen. She seemed to have a true sense of accomplishment that motivated her to go on.

It is important to note that in this family the mother reinforced her daughters' use of LOGO.

Sometimes, however, the children who spoke as if they liked to use word processing and other educational software did not seem to make much use of it. In other words, some children talked about using the computer for educational purposes, but evidence showed that they mainly used the computer for games. For example, one twelve-year-old girl reported benefiting from the math software she used in school and using educational software with a friend: "After school, my close friend who likes computers comes over and we practice what we've learned during that day. She brings her math software with her. And then we practice for a few hours – it's fun." She claimed to have positive feelings about word processing, too. However, this family estimated that 90 percent of computer use was for games.[3]

In the main, children's intense interest in computer games made their interest in educational software pale by comparison. Their lack of positive experiences with academic software increasingly lowered their receptivity to it and also contributed to their subsequent lack of effort in educational computing. The perceptions and expectations children and parents had of computers may also have contributed to this state of affairs.

THE COMPUTER AS TOY: NEGATIVE AND POSITIVE ASPECTS

The conceptions that children and parents had about computers may have contributed to their acceptance of computer gaming and their rejection of educational software. Frequently their conceptions were conveyed through the language they used when talking about computers. In this section, as in Chapter 6, considerable emphasis is placed on the words they used to describe what they thought about computers.

To many children and their parents, the computer was mainly a game machine. A thirteen-year-old boy, upon being asked about his plans for future use of the computer, thought that he would "do more [word processing] projects and play games. . . . There is nothing else to do on it." In spite of having used academic software, Andrew Quarles, when asked what he thought a computer was good for, responded, "It is good to play games on." The use of academic software had not changed his perception of computers.

To many, the computer was more than a game machine; it was also an intriguing "toy" with which one could "play" and have "fun." The word "play" could refer to game playing, to programming activities ("Programming is exciting, interesting; it's also a lot of fun"), and to other uses of the computer. Although more males seemed intrigued by the computer than

127

females, both sexes recognized the attraction. It was revealing to see how frequently parents and children referred to the computer as a "toy" and how often they used the words "play" and "fun" when speaking about it. The computer was "Daddy's toy" and a toy for children. A five-year-old boy who liked "to play computer" declared, "I like computers because they're fun." Sometimes the words "toy" and "play" were used to approve of the user's fascination with the computer, while at other times they were used pejoratively to criticize the use.

Many fathers tinkered with the computer because they were captivated by it. A few enjoyed programming. Some derived enjoyment from using the computer for work-related activities; for them, the computer made work play. One father declared, "Doing taxes is fun, when you use the computer!" while another reported, "I use the computer for fun. The data base, for example, I play with numbers, data, inventories. It is a game for me to make a list of grades for students."

As seen in Chapter 6, the fact that some mothers conceived of computers as toys meant that they did not feel obligated to use computers themselves. A fieldworker thought one mother's intonation suggested "that what she did was more important at least in her estimation. She used the word 'play,' which confirmed my idea that she thought that time spent with the computer was probably not important time."

Many parents thought the computer was an expensive and useless toy for their children and doubted that it could be of any real use to them; "Right now they're an expensive toy" was a typical comment. Deep down, these parents did not see a relationship between computer use and education. On the contrary, instead of associating computer use with learning, they perceived a dichotomy between the two. In addition, they did not think that learning could be fun, nor did they connect the idea of play with educational computing. As one mother declared, "Now they just play around – it's more fun to them than learning."

In a few instances, parents who disapproved of excessive game playing and who did not understand how children could benefit educationally from computers made rules putting schoolwork ahead of computer play. These rules served to work against the use of computers for educational purposes. As one fieldworker recorded, an eighth-grader "revealed that he tended to get his homework done faster since the computer served as an enticement, something that he was allowed to use when he was finished."

In an extreme case, a daughter spoke about her father's view: "My father says that the computer is for fun and that schoolwork is serious." The father stuck rigidly to his rule that homework had to be completed before his children could use the computer. He claimed that he had had to make it because his children were playing games on the computer but the twelve-year-old daughter claimed that she wanted to use the computer to do her English homework and was not allowed to do so. She was one of the few children in the study who seemed to have a conception of the power of using a word processor: "The best part is moving pieces of my compositions around without having to rewrite the whole thing." Her four-teen-year-old brother, stimulated by his sister's desire to word process, tried to convince his father to let him use the word processor to do his English homework. His father's main reaction was, "When your grades in English go up and you prove that you deserve it, then you can use it for English homework, too. Not 'til then! . . . No toy, no matter how expensive it is can make your grades go up."

As is obvious in this last example, the rules parents made about computer use often served to accentuate further the wide gulf between using the home computer for educational and for recreational purposes; they also fostered the conception that computers were toys and thus were separate from learning. Instead of attempting to lead their children toward constructive, educational computer use, instead of trying to show their children that computers were not just toys but were machines that could be used for educational purposes, the parents who made rules reinforced the conception of the computer as a game machine to be used after schoolwork was finished.

Only in a few families did a parent make a comment to the effect that it was good to have fun while learning. "It's a toy to them but it's an educational toy, a learning tool," was one mother's comment. A father declared, "There isn't anything wrong with the laughter. If it helps kids learn, it's OK." But in most of these instances, parents seemed to be paying lip service to the value of educational computer use. Most did nothing to expand their children's view of the computer from educational toy to enjoyable learning tool.

Mrs. Lawrence was one of the few parents who realized and supported the intellectual value of play on the computer. She acknowledged that when her daughters were using the computer to program in LOGO they were engaging in cognitive play: "A lot of cognitive play goes on." She supported their endeavors. When asked if she supplemented what the children did in school, she answered, "They do a lot of cognitive play and when I see that, I reinforce it." She spoke about watching one of her daughters using LOGO:

> One day for several hours, Patricia sat down upstairs and she used only right angles and increments of ten. . . . She was experimenting with F 10, R 90. F 20, R 90. It was not premeditated, but structured in that there was a theme. . . . I sat back and watched and thought, "That's a cognitive activity." I can't think of a parallel activity without the computer that she does. She doesn't know that these are angles, but when she encounters formal geometry there will be groundwork and she won't have to memorize certain things. And she does this for fun. . . . It's enjoyable. It's like a game and yet it's putting certain building blocks about spatial relationships.

On the whole, children exhibited a game attitude toward computers, and parents showed, at best, an ambivalence about the educational uses of computers. Although some of the parents came close to articulating how computers can be used for learning, they were probably a long way from really believing it or understanding how their children could benefit educationally from computers. Just as children had no one to show them or model for them how computers could be used for educational purposes, so parents had no one to show them or model for them such educational use. In addition, parents gave little serious thought to how using computers can make learning more enjoyable; in other words, parents did not recognize the value of play for learning or the role computers could have in their children's education. In fact, the view of the computer as toy, as plaything, may have kept them from really wanting their children to use the computer for learning instead of promoting their interest in doing so.

NOTES

1. By studying the factors that seem to affect the attraction of games and the aversion to educational software, we may learn something about creating motivating educational software and environments in which such software is used. In addition, interest in video games leads to a consideration of the role of intrinsic motivation and play in learning and to how expectations affect what and how people learn from using technology.
2. The father of another family felt differently about computer games: "After a while, I think a lot of those games claw on you. There's just so much zapping and flags popping up or blimps or whatever. It's boring after a while. It has to be boring."
3. Even when children's actions did not support statements of receptivity to educational software, there is a positive aspect to these remarks. By making a favorable comment about educational computer use, even if they do not actually engage in much educational computing, children indicate that they have a certain openness toward doing so. Making a positive statement could be the first step, a step that parents and teachers could nurture.

Chapter 9

Redefining a New Technology as a
Social Innovation

> Change is not slowed simply because people like the status quo ante,
> or even because they fear uncertainty. . . . Often it is blocked because
> people fail to create good new ways of acting, thinking, and relating to
> each other. (Calhoun, 1981, p. 422)

In this chapter and the two that follow, we discuss three
broad lessons emerging from our study, lessons indicating
that new technologies should be viewed as social innovations. We start with the point that educational computer use
at home – or for that matter the use of any technology in any
setting – requires a compatible "social envelope," if promised outcomes such as children's mastery of academic subject matter or computer tool skills are to occur. Our findings
suggest that these educational promises have not been met
in part because parents and children lack a clear image of the
needed social envelope. Their lack of vision is due in large
measure to the neglect of these social behaviors and relations, especially by advocates of home educational computing. Therefore, one broad lesson of our research is that
creators and promoters will need to develop clearer visions
or images of effective home envelopes if they want to encourage children, with the cooperation of their parents, to
engage in serious educational computing.

In this chapter, we explore the social-envelope concept and
relate our findings to it. We then propose ways to develop
clearer images of social envelopes for effective home educational computing.

132

OUR FIELDWORK FINDINGS AND
THEIR IMPLICATIONS

As pointed out in Chapters 4 and 5, the parents we studied had little awareness or understanding of available educational software. Also, many did not see any value in its use for their children. In Chapter 5, we demonstrated that few parents appreciated the leadership role they would need to assume at home and, in Chapter 6, that the orientation of most mothers toward computers was especially counterproductive. In Chapter 7, we showed how the connection with the school affected children's educational computer activities at home and parents' expectations as well; the overall effect was not positive. And in Chapter 8, we reported that few children and their siblings or friends acknowledged the potential educational functions of the computer. In short, most parents and their children lacked clear and positive images of the roles they would have to play in order to engage successfully in educational computing at home.

The opposite was true in the instances where home educational computing did occur – for example, in the regular use of academic software in the Quarles family or the less frequent use of LOGO in the Lawrence family. Parent and child actions in these and a few other families indicated the presence of positive visions of educational computing. In these instances, parents found productive and rewarding ways for their children to use software educationally. In their roles with their children, especially younger children, they engaged in such forms of educational interaction as modeling, coaching, and scaffolding; they did not expect the machine to simply take over the educational process by sitting children in front of it. They required children to put forth considerable direct effort; they did not expect learning on the computer to be all fun or to be easy. They themselves became computer learners.

These parents gave priority (even if it was just temporary, as in the sporadic cases) to their children's computing efforts; they expected to spend time and effort. They expected to shoulder and, in fact, took responsibility for such matters as choosing (at times in collaboration with their children) appropriate software, and setting computer goals and overseeing their accomplishment. These parents initiated and maintained direct communication with their children's schools about computing. They tried to create a space at home that would be conducive to their children's educational computing. Children in these families expected to and did devote considerable effort and mindful attention to their computing for academic or other educational purposes. They did this in cooperation with parents and at times with siblings or friends, not alone.

Our findings strongly suggest that the kind and extent of educational computing occurring at home depended on the social expectations about educational goals and behavior prevailing in the family. We turn now to a discussion of these social expectations, which in their entirety form a "social envelope" that surrounds and shapes a technology's use.[1]

A TECHNOLOGY'S SOCIAL ENVELOPE:
A METAPHOR

Advocates of technological innovation often seem to focus their attention on the technology itself and on the goals they believe the technology can accomplish. They do not give enough attention to the beliefs and behaviors that need to accompany a technology in order for it to have the desired effects. These are assumed to simply follow once the technology is introduced and are treated as secondary or are overlooked. In effect, those who are technology-oriented say, "Let's just introduce the technology. In the process, the technology will change people as needed."

Those of us who take a social-organizational perspective, however, view this technological emphasis as misplaced. Our perspective does not treat the technology per se as the primary focus. For us the heart of the innovation does not reside in the technology or even its goals. Instead, it is to be found in the attitudes and activities that people need to adopt before they can use the technology to achieve specific goals.[2]

Mehan (1989, p. 19), in discussing computers in schools, echoes the need to focus on the social side of technology:

> A microcomputer in a classroom is a social practice and not a technology. The crucial ingredient is people's experience with the machine, not its "inherent" features. It is what people do with the machine, not the machine itself, that makes a difference.

Similarly, Salomon and Gardner (1986, pp. 17–18) argue that "computers do not really affect learners in any direct way; it is the way they *are used* [our emphasis] that is crucial."

Let us take this social emphasis one step further. The social situations into which technologies are introduced are often referred to as contexts, settings, or environments. Such places have existing norms[3] or expectations for what goals, role behavior, interaction, beliefs, values, and attitudes *ought to be*.[4] These social expectations, which people hold, surround or envelop a technology when it is introduced and in so doing they shape the way people use it, if they use it at all. Salomon (1986, p. 14) articulates the fundamental effect of social expectations on computer use in the following way: "Socially agreed-upon notions, cultural conventions, and shared meanings play a major role. . . . [They] affect the way computers are approached, the sustained effort expended, and the tasks individuals choose for activity."

Left unaltered, the existing social envelope – the configuration of social expectations or arrangements that envelop a technology – lead people to use the technology in a way that closely conforms to existing purposes (Bork, 1985; Kepner, 1986; Naisbitt, 1982; Salomon and Gardner, 1986). Today, children use home computers most often as game machines that have replaced the Atari and Intellivision sets of the late 1970s or as word processors for school papers in place of the manual and electric typewriters that came before them.

If, for its effective use, a new technology requires role behavior, interaction, and beliefs that deviate greatly from those prescribed by the existing social envelope, then the only way to ensure its desired use is to change the envelope.[5] As Scott, Cole, and Engel (1992, p. 196) write:

> One of the few firm laws concerning the effects of introducing a new technology is the tendency of the social system to retain current goals and social organizations. . . . To be successful as an agent of change (*re*form), technologically based strategies should be based in a *self-conscious effort to construct a social environment with a new morphology of interpersonal communication*. (Our emphasis)

Before an envelope can be changed in preferred ways, a clear vision of those changes must be present. Most people become stymied without such an image. The social-organizational perspective requires first and foremost a focus on the nature of the existing social envelope and on the ways that this envelope must be changed *at the time* the technology is introduced.[6] Without serious attention to the shape of the desired envelope, a technology will not be used in its most innovative and promising ways except by chance, especially at the beginning.

Parenthetically, even if one has an explicit vision of the new social envelope, it does not mean that people's behavior will conform to it. A clear conception is not tantamount to its enactment. The difficult and equally social matter of enacting or implementing a new social envelope will be taken up in Chapter 10. Our study, suffice it to say here, suggests that the vast majority of today's families have little or no vision of what a proper envelope for educational home computing would look like for them. Similarly, schools do not have a clear view of educational home computing, or for that matter a clear image of what educational computing can or should be at school (Levin, 1990).

To take our thinking about social envelopes one step further, expectations surrounding a technology can be differentiated into at least three overlapping layers: individual hands-on, social-interactive, and social-ecological expectations. These layers affect each other, and taken together they determine whether a technology will achieve a specific end once introduced. In any given setting, one layer might be more fully envisioned than the other two. How this affects the actual use of a technology remains to be determined through site-specific research. However, it seems reasonable to suppose that all layers need to be conceptualized and then their presence ensured if the desired use, in quantity and quality, of a technology is to be achieved.

THE HANDS-ON LAYER

At the center of any appropriate social envelope are the expectations that describe an individual's direct use of a technology. This can be characterized as the "hands-on" layer of the envelope. Tornatzky and his associates (1983, p. 7), in an extensive review of technological innovation, employ the term "embedding content" to refer to such expectations.[7] Using the example of the sewing machine in a garment factory, they note:

> Certain changes in operator behavior are necessary in order to use this machine. The embedding content consists at least of the sewers' learning how to thread the machine, feed the material, etc. – all the behaviors necessary in order to operate the new machines. The technology is thus represented by *both* the machine and the behaviors necessary to operate the machinery.

We would add that at this level there are also expectations regarding the user's values, attitudes, and beliefs about the direct use of a particular technology. In the area of educational computing, hardware and software creators are probably most aware of this layer, focused as they are on the behavior of the individual in front of the computer.

THE SOCIAL INTERACTION LAYER

Surrounding this person-to-machine layer is the "social interaction" layer, which contains expectations about the patterns of interaction that users in a given setting need to engage in. These patterns prescribe interaction, often with nonusers, in order to achieve desired ends with a technology. Many creators of educational software appear to spend little or no time embedding expectations related to this interaction layer into their software or software guides.[8] Although some may be aware of the importance of this layer, most creators need to give greater attention to it. The same can be said for proponents of educational computing in general.

THE SOCIAL ECOLOGY LAYER

Surrounding these two concentric layers of expectations – the person-to-machine and the person-to-person – is the "social ecology" layer. This layer contains overarching expectations about the purposes, structure, and resources of a given setting – human, physical, technological, and other material conditions – available for a technology's use. This layer also includes the expectations for how the setting in question should relate to other social units. Software creators and other champions of home educational computing need to give far more conscious attention to this layer of the social envelope.

DEVELOPING VISIONS OF
EDUCATIONAL COMPUTING

Some investigators of educational computing have recognized the need for adequately articulated social envelopes. Sheingold, Hawkins, and Char (1984, p. 2) early on acknowledged the importance of focusing on classroom social arrangements. In writing about drill and practice, programming, word processing, and data base management, they emphasized:

> Each of these uses may have different ways of fitting into and shaping the work of the classroom, as well as the patterns of social interaction surrounding that work. . . . We need to ask about particular uses of the technology in order to begin to understand its relation to the social life of classrooms.

Tom Snyder, of Snyder Productions – an educational software company – put it another way: "We're going to miss the boat unless we recognize that any innovation in the school will fail if it does not take into account the complex social environment of a school" (cited in Lewis, 1988, p. 15).

Unfortunately, the above observations focus on schools, not homes. Moreover, *recognizing* the need for clear images is not enough.[9] There still remains the thorny task of *building* effective visions, which at present do not exist for homes.[10]

Effective visions can best be developed by those who experimentally apply various learning theories to computer use or who observe at length what occurs naturally in real settings.[11] One example of an experimentally oriented researcher is Harel. Her work is steeped in the thinking of such learning theoreticians as Piaget, Vygotsky, Perkins, and especially Papert. Harel states that her work has focused on developing a model for Papert's theory of constructionism by "allowing each child to learn concepts in fractions and Logo through his or her (concrete and abstract) own construction of an interactive teaching device – at the same time allowing this process of building and abstractions to be influenced by the child's interactions and conversations with the peers who were around him or her, doing the same job and involved in similar processes" (Harel, 1991, p. 32). We see this as a theoretically based effort that might ultimately establish key expectations of one potentially effective envelope for educational computing, expectations for both the hands-on and social interaction layers.

Carroll (1990) is yet another among the group of applied researchers trying to create theory-based models of computer use that would achieve various cognitive and affective goals. Some of his research focuses on determining the minimum amount of instruction beginning computer users need in order to get going. Again, we view the possible outcome of this work as the stipulation of hands-on expectations, though not labeled as such, necessary for the effective start-up of beginning computer users. He emphasizes that the essence of the minimalist approach (we would say of the social envelope) "is to obstruct as little as possible the learner's self-initiated efforts to find meaning in the activities of learning." He points out that this happens "by supporting the rapid achievement of realistic projects even from the start of training . . . and by designing for error recognition and recovery as basic instructional events" (p. xvii).

Generated largely in university settings and research and development centers, applied research of the above kind has the potential, since it is theory driven, of explaining why an envelope needs to have a certain shape as well as why, when enacted, it has the effects observed. As Nickerson (1991, p. 24) acknowledges, however, "the work of the laboratory has not had the beneficial impact on approaches to teaching and training, in either educational or industrial contexts, that one would hope and expect it to have."[12] This work also has the potential drawback, for our purposes, of emphasizing educational computing *in schools.* Its relevance by analogy to *home* computing envelopes seems clear. However, the two settings differ in their purposes, status arrangements, and role structures. Hence, the actual value of this applied research will depend upon future attempts to use school-based findings in the development of home envelopes.

Research and writing bearing directly on home envelopes is almost nonexistent. This does not mean that popular books, computer magazines, and software guides offer no suggestions about how children and parents can use their home computers for education. As a matter of fact, a great deal has been written on these subjects. Blank and Berlin (1991, pp. 375–83), for example, offer answers to common questions about setting up a home computer center in their recent parental guide to educational software. Recast as basic expectations for a vision of home educational computing, their recommendations deal with computer placement and work space; software awareness and purchase; general habits of computer and software care; the parental role in their children's computer activities such as helping, supporting, and monitoring children's daily computer routines and purposes; and parental communication with the school. Yet, their "image" and that of many software developers and other popular writers (e.g., Plummer and Bowman, 1988; Olsen, 1988; Polley and Wenn, 1988) is one of children working independently at the computer. More important, these "images" are piecemeal, limited, and without recognizable theoretical or research backing.

Ultimately, any vision of effective educational computing – whether for the home or for school – will need to provide full descriptions of (1) the computer activities children would be engaged in, (2) when and how often children would be so engaged, (3) with whom and in what surroundings (social, material, and physical) these activities would take place, and (4) what goal(s) these activities would be aimed at achieving. It will also have to offer an explanation for why and how these activities and surroundings, so constructed, would achieve the desired goals. Moreover, many factors will no doubt modify the shape that an effective social envelope for educational computing would take. These include: the ages of children; gender; number of children; learning needs and goals; learning strengths and styles; parental and child computer expertise; prevailing software, hardware, and physical features of the workplace; and the time available to family members.

OTHER CONSIDERATIONS IN THE
BUILDING OF HOME ENVELOPES

A number of other considerations accompany envelope building. We sketch out several that seem to be particularly salient for creators and other proponents of home computing.

LOOSE AND TIGHT SOCIAL ENVELOPES

Developers and other proponents may not be able to make desirable social envelopes for home or for school computing *totally* explicit. Using the example of the sewing machine factory, Tornatzky and his associates (1983, p. 7) put it this way: "Much of the embedding content [his term for part of the social envelope] will only become 'revealed' during the process of implementation (for example, what to do with the production line when the machines break down)." But "loose shapes" can be created. With experience and with appropriate help, a family (or a school) could adapt or tailor a loose-fitting shape into a home-specific (or school-specific) "tight shape."

DIFFERENT ENVELOPES FOR
DIFFERENT PURPOSES

In this chapter, we posit that the technology itself determines only part of what the social envelope must be and that the desired use of the machine shapes a great deal more. This means that the same machine may necessitate substantially different social envelopes – social innovations – if substantially different uses are pursued.[13] Even if we restrict our analysis of home computers to their use for educational purposes, markedly different envelopes seem probable. To begin with, the use of the computer as an educational tutor with academic software represents a different innovation from its use as an educational tool (e.g., word processing) or a tutee (e.g., programming). Although there are some common expectations such as keyboarding at the hands-on level, expectations about the style and amount of keyboarding differ among the three layers. Even within the area of academic computing, the use of different software packages could require substantially different expectations, especially for the hands-on layer.

The specific role expectations between children and parents at the social interaction level also seem to differ, depending upon use. Learning to program the computer or learning to word process school papers may require different kinds of encouragement and assistance from parents than academic computing. At the social ecology level, academic computing would require that parents provide children with appropriately updated software as they master work on earlier disks. The continued awareness and purchase of new software would not be as pronounced in the case of word processing or programming. At the same time, ergonomic expectations might not differ that much across purposes.

THE STUDY OF THE UNSPOKEN WORD

Often fundamental expectations about home envelopes are conveyed not in spoken or written words but in pictures or images. The cover of the aforementioned Blank and Berlin book, for instance, shows a brother and sister at the computer, with their father standing behind them. The father is pointing to the screen in what could be interpreted as an "instructional" gesture. All three seem to be enjoying the computer experience very much.[14]

Happy posing of this kind – usually including two parents – has been repeated in home computer and educational software advertisements and on television throughout the past decade. Families always seem to look happy and comfortable with the machine and seem to know what to do with it. What expectations do such pictures convey? How realistic or accurate are they? Ideally, what should family members be saying to each other? How should they relate to each other when using the keyboard, joystick, or mouse with particular software? What effects have such portrayals had on parental images of educational computing at home? Future research will need to focus on answering these kinds of questions.

THE NEED FOR MORE SOCIAL MEDIATION RESEARCH

The development of educational software certainly needs to go beyond the simplistic message conveyed to parents: buy the software; sit the children in front of it; and then, stand away, stand aside, or stand by and let the machine take over! As noted earlier, full descriptions of home or school envelopes should be guided not only by the common sense and practical experience of the software developer but also by the promising theories of educators and researchers who are involved in instructional design and learning.

Much of the work mentioned in this chapter supports the position that learning occurs through socially mediated interactions. ·Vygotsky (1978), especially, proposes that parents can create a set of conditions for learning, which he calls "the zone of proximal development." This learning zone is the space between what an individual already knows and what he or she can learn to do with help, especially in interaction with "a more competent other" (Polin, 1991). It seems likely that a dynamic of this sort was operative to some degree in the few families, such as the Quarles and Lawrence families, in which children, in collaboration with a parent, were using computers for educational purposes. But, in order for software or guides for parents to be theory based, developers would first need to understand thoroughly the theory. They would then need to use it consciously in their research and development software efforts, notwithstanding the difficulties of working with families in naturalistic settings or under laboratory conditions.

A FINAL NOTE ON VISIONS OF HOME EDUCATIONAL COMPUTING

The new expectations necessary in all three layers of a setting's social envelope are the essence of a technological innovation. Our purpose in this chapter has not been to propose an impossible task: the explicit predetermination of all the new social expectations to be enacted. Rather, we have tried to show that what is needed is complex and that even some rather simple actions in developing desirable home envelopes would help foster educational computing at home. If computing is to have an empowering influence on families, especially in the education of children, then key players – software developers and other proponents – will have to stop defining home educational computing in terms of hardware and software. They will have to begin viewing it in the framework of human behavior and recognize that it requires new patterns of social interaction and communication, which means change, at least in part, in the home's social envelope.

NOTES

1. For several reasons we chose the social envelope metaphor to depict the social milieu in any setting that surrounds a technology. First, it simplifies what is an extremely complex set of social forces too unwieldy to deal with in their entirety in most discussions. Second, and more important, this metaphor permits one to grasp the relationship between a new technology and the setting into which it is introduced. In many ways, introducing a new technology is just like placing a letter in an envelope. A

letter or card must be shaped in ways that allow it to enter the shape of the existing envelope, or a new envelope must be provided. The metaphor aptly conveys what usually happens to a technology when it is introduced into a social setting. It either fits or something must give – either the letter (the technological use) or the envelope (the social expectations and relations of the setting).

2. Turning away from the technological object itself and toward its functions and uses, one is led to ask different questions, such as: Is the technology being used and if so, how? How do we want the technology to be used? What is the optimal social context if the technology is to be used for a particular purpose? What must the new expectations for behavior and interaction be? Put another way, what role changes are necessary?

3. We use the term "norm" to mean group standards for what behavior and thought should be. We are not using it to mean actual average behavior or thought, although these two phenomena overlap considerably in settings with minimal deviance.

4. Social scientists often label these social arrangements and values as a setting's social structure or culture. For several early treatments of social structure and culture, see Blau and Scott (1962) and Gross, Mason, and McEachern (1958). The social structure and culture of a school or family setting has been specified variously as a set of values, mores, and purposes; a set of statuses and roles; a division of labor; a system of communication; a process of decision making; and an authority structure or a system of power. For a current discussion of the concept of culture as applied to schools, see Erickson (1991, pp. 1–12). Ost (1991, p. 79) most succinctly states that culture "is generally described in terms of observable, socially transmitted *patterns of behavior*" (emphasis his) and that these "are manifestations of basic elements responsible for culture (beliefs, values, expectations, etc.)." He then points out: "In this sense culture must be thought of *as ideas or rules that direct the behavior of its members*" (emphasis ours). We would add that these ideas or rules cluster differentially around the statuses or positions found in any setting and as such are called "roles." We refer to the above social features of a setting metaphorically as the social envelope.

5. How much of any social envelope requires changing when a new technology is introduced depends on whether the existing arrangements are compatible with the desired use of the tech-

nology. In general, quite a few expectations existing in a setting would affect a technology's use directly and, as such, would need to be altered. Others, and depending upon the machine and its desired use perhaps most, would not impinge upon use directly. But many of these might in some way or another be indirectly related. There is really no telling ahead of time how much of an original envelope needs to be changed for a machine to be effectively used to achieve desired ends.

6. While we shall maintain this position, we are also aware that technologies originally constructed in one way are often changed in order to accommodate the existing structure if they are tried out and found to be incompatible or incomplete in some ways. For example, while the computer's basic structure has not changed much during these past ten years, there have been big changes in memory (size and type) and ancillary machinery that make them somewhat easier to use or to use more effectively.

7. They borrowed this term from Pelz and Munson.

8. This is not to say that all creators are oblivious to the need to address this area of computer use. For example, Peter Reynolds of Tom Snyder Productions indicates that their philosophy is to encourage group experiences with the computer and to try to help children and parents see the computer as a place where several people can gather. In elucidating what he means, Reynolds is reported as saying that when one person sitting next to another says, "Here's what that means," those at Tom Snyder Associates believe that "a deeper learning groove" is made in one's brain (as cited in Lewis, 1992, p. C7).

9. There are a number of overarching labels for educational computing in schools. The longest standing is that of "computer-assisted instruction" (CAI). Another treats the computer as the instructional centerpiece of the classroom and school and goes by the name "computer-based instruction" (CBI). A more current label is integrated learning systems (ILS). And still another is "computer-managed instruction" (CMI). These and other views, which lack such recognized acronyms, treat the computer variously as dominant or ancillary to instruction in the classroom. These labels and others, however, do not offer clear visions of the envelopes that would need to surround school computing. For a brief treatment of these labels, see Scott, Cole, and Engel (1992, pp. 206–12).

10. For an excellent discussion of visions of computer use for classrooms, see the symposium included in the *Harvard Educational*

Review, vol. 59, no. 1 (February 1989), pp. 50–85, and responses to the symposium included in vol. 59, no. 2 (May 1989), pp. 206–25.

11. Scott, Cole, and Engel (1992, pp. 220–43) provide an excellent over-view of certain promising research efforts, including the Apple Classroom of Tomorrow (ACOT) and Apple Global Education (AGE) by Apple Computer Inc.; The Jasper Project by Vanderbilt's Cognition and Technology Group; Earth Lab by members of Bolt, Beranek, and Newman; work at MIT's Media Lab, especially on LOGO; and the work of the University of California's Laboratory of Comparative Human Cognition (LCHC).

12. Indeed, the typical effort of teachers and administrators to shape computing in their schools seems to reflect their own practical and too often atheoretical and idiosyncratic expectations. Most "visions" appear to be a function of the availability of resources – time, energy, materials – and the "gut" reactions of teachers and students to the technology rather than the result of learning and instructional theory or research. Incidentally, a fair reading of the extant school computer literature suggests that the over-whelming focus has been on reporting the *effects* of school com-puter use, not on thorough descriptions of the social envelopes proposed and enacted during these efforts.

13. To illustrate by analogy: the use of the automobile for the pur-pose of family transportation requires quite a different set of expected behaviors and attitudes than would its use for drag racing, even though some behaviors and attitudes would be common to both uses. The *same* machine or technology, in other words, can be associated with many *different* social envelopes.

14. Curiously, the mother is not present on the Blank and Berlin cover. While this squares with what we found in most SITE families, does this picture have the effect of promoting – probab-ly unintentionally – the expectation that mothers "need not apply" for the role of coach or scaffolder for children's home computing? This is ironic given the fact that most often it is the mother, not the father, who is expected to be involved in their children's educational efforts at school and at home. This in-volvement has to do with monitoring school progress in general and with specific activities such as helping with or overseeing the completion of homework assignments. The mother's greater involvement is especially relevant when it comes to the many families with single heads of households, which are nearly all

female directed. Moreover, our study suggests that such a differential gender expectation is counterproductive to serious educational computing efforts, since in the several families where there was purposeful educational computing – e.g., the Quarles and the Lawrence families – it was the mothers who spearheaded children's computer efforts.

Chapter 10

Viewing Technological Change as a Social Process

Change is a process, not an event . . . a lesson learned the hard way by those who put all their energies into developing an innovation...without thinking through what would have to happen beyond that point. (Fullan, 1991, p. 49)

We argued earlier that the effective use of a technology requires a clear vision of an appropriate social envelope, a point that policy makers and advocates of home computers for education tend to miss.[1] However, clear visions of home computing are not enough. In this chapter, we argue that such visions have to be enacted in homes. They do not occur automatically, as the technologically minded so often seem to assume, by simply "letting the technology loose."

A second broad lesson of our research is that creators and champions of home educational computing need to view the effective use of a technology as the consequence of a multi-staged, social process of diffusion, adoption, and then implementation. The evidence uncovered by our study suggests that most "strategies" used by marketers or advocates to get educational software and hardware into homes are seriously flawed. Their strategies often limit diffusion, curtail adoption, or overlook the problematic nature of implementation. The prevailing "here it is, buy it" and then "simply do it" approach may work for the occasional or passionately proactive family. It is not sufficient for most others.

In this chapter, we review our findings in light of the aforementioned steps in the planned change process. We also discuss their implications for developing more effective strategies of change, if children's educational computing efforts at home are to be fostered or rekindled.

Historically, the focus on the diffusion and adoption of innovations – the spread of a new idea and the decision to try it – came first (Arensberg and Niehoff, 1964; Barnett, 1953; Fliegel and Kivlin, 1966; Mort, 1953; Rogers, 1962; Spicer, 1952). The implementation of innovations – the enactment of new ideas in local settings – has been a more recent concern (Fullan, 1991; Gross, Giacquinta, and Bernstein, 1971; Huberman and Miles, 1984; Sarason, 1990).[2]

DIFFUSION

Alcorn (1986, p. 98) describes what often happens during the early diffusion of a new technology:

> At first . . . a product is presented with much fanfare, and an advertising campaign is designed to put the name and image of the product before the public as often and as well as possible. This creates an awareness of the product in the minds of potential consumers.

In spreading the news about a new idea, word-of-mouth is probably as important, if not more so, than commercial advertising. Indeed, many creators seem to depend primarily upon the "did you hear about it" approach because they do not have the financial resources to mount large-scale advertising campaigns. Free advertising occurs when innovations are written about in newspapers and magazines or talked about on radio or television. It is no wonder, therefore, that the change literature stresses "social location" (not to be mistaken with social status) as being critical to explaining why some potential adopters know about a certain innovation and others do not. Those in the "right place at the right time" learn about it.

Providing knowledge about an innovation is not enough. An effective diffusion strategy has to communicate not only the existence of an innovation but also its importance in meeting a "felt" need, which potential adopters have. If there is little or no "felt" need within the target audience, then adoption is blocked because interest – a second key in the process of adoption – will not be created.[3]

As we saw, most parents had little or no awareness of existing educational software, and they had little interest in using it with their children. We would argue that these two conditions – little or no awareness and interest – were due in part to the fact that most creators and advocates of software had little or no way of making parents aware of their "products" and of convincing them that these would meet an important family need. The story for computer hardware is a bit different. In contrast to software, there are but a handful of basic computers and a relatively small amount of ancillary hardware. The computer companies with very large budgets have been able to mount more successful diffusion and adoption efforts. Here we use "successful" only to mean that the rate of computer sales, hence the *fact* of adoption, is enormous compared with the sales of most software.[4]

ADOPTION

Rogers's (1983) extensive analysis of adoption covers hundreds of studies in such areas as agriculture, anthropology, business, education, health, and medicine. According to his adoption curve, as the news about an innovation spreads across a target population of potential users, adoption – the decision to try the change – follows a curve composed of five categories: innovators, early adopters, early majority, late majority, and laggards (Rogers, 1983, p. 205).[5]

As in the case of diffusion, the adoption of educational computing is a complex matter. There are many adoption possibilities. Moreover, a family could be an "early adopter" of one piece of software, a "laggard" on several others, and fall into the "never adopt" category for all the others. As we found in our study, many families did not adopt any educational software; nearly all of those remaining adopted just a few pieces.

While awareness and interest are critical to adoption, several other conditions are also pivotal: whether potential adopters can try out the innovation (in our case, software and hardware), whether the innovation can be shown to be effective, and whether potential adopters can financially afford the innovation. Change strategies that do not take these conditions into account – along with spreading the news and fostering interest – reduce the likelihood that an innovation will be adopted by most of the target population.

Our study suggests that most software promoter strategies failed to provide for the adequate trial of their programs. These strategies did not convey convincingly that the software, if used, would be effective. Moreover, without trial possibilities and demonstrated effectiveness, a typical piece of software becomes a risky investment. Add this to the fact that children's educational computing at home would require quite a few different programs, and the cost of software becomes clearly high for the average family. Prevailing strategies have not taken this into account either.

IMPLEMENTATION

Even when an innovation is adopted, its use in the desired way cannot be assumed. The absence of educational and especially academic computing within families that *had* proper software and hardware makes this point clear. Those who focus their change efforts on diffusion and adoption truncate the change process. They leave open or take on faith the actual nature and extent of an innovation's *utilization*.

Carlson (1965), in his study of the adoption of three educational innovations by school systems located in three states, provides a classic illustration. After an extensive quantitative analysis of the adoption of the innovations (as reported by school system superintendents), he completes his work with a chapter entitled "Unanticipated Consequences in the Use of Programmed Instruction." In this chapter, Carlson (1965, p. 78) presents a qualitative analysis of this innovation in one school setting and makes the following observation:

Programmed instruction, possibly more than any other innovation, presents the teacher and the school with the opportunity of achieving individualized instruction. However, when this opportunity presented itself in this single case, certain mechanisms emerged, such as restricting the pace of fast learners and allowing slower students more time to work on programs, which tended to minimize the spread of progress through the program by students of varying ability.

What Carlson called "unanticipated consequences" and the "emergence of certain mechanisms," we would define as the degree to which the innovation was implemented or adapted to local conditions. Given the fact that the innovation had already been diffused and adopted, what he demonstrated in this case study was that the promise of programmed instruction was being undermined at the local level by teachers who were to implement it.

The Carlson study deals with organizational change. It provides an important conceptual bridge that helps one understand what happened to the home computer and to educational and especially academic computing in our study. From this organizational perspective, the family, like the school, is a social system and the adoption of an innovation in a family or school is an effort by a person or group inside or outside the system to introduce change.

Consequently, a technology cannot be introduced into a social setting without the coordinated efforts of many individuals, and adoption must be followed by a number of conditions and member actions if it is to be properly used or implemented. Also, a technology's initiator or adopter may not be and often is not the actual user or implementer.[6] In our study, while parents were the computer adopters, their children were expected to be focal, educational implementers – of course, still with the coordinated support efforts of parents and others.

In sum, advocates of educational home computing need to recognize that the effective use of a technology, even when adopted, remains problematic. Implementation, the next step in the planned change process, does not flow automatically from adoption.

CONDITIONS BEHIND SUCCESSFUL IMPLEMENTATION

Let us turn now to the conditions that facilitate an innovation's implementation. We focus in particular on the characteristics of the potential implementers and the existing change setting.

CHARACTERISTICS OF THE IMPLEMENTERS

Implementation depends in part on the characteristics of those who must carry out an innovation. The features most discussed in the planned change literature are implementer receptivity, skill, and understanding.

Receptivity. Most change agents and researchers see implementer receptivity as one of the key elements in the successful enactment of an innovation. McLaughlin (1987, p. 172) emphasizes this point in explaining why policy makers have so much difficulty getting potential implementers to try something new:

> It's hard to make something happen primarily because policy-makers can't mandate what matters. We have learned that policy success depends critically on two broad factors: local capacity and will. Capacity, admittedly a difficult issue, is something that policy can address. Training can be offered. Dollars can be provided. Consultants can be engaged to furnish missing expertise. But will, or the attitudes, motivation, and beliefs that underlie an implementor's response to a policy's goals or strategies, is less amenable to policy intervention.

In our study, family members expressed different feelings, but most resisted carrying out new expectations related to educational computing. Some family members were adamantly against the purchase and use of home computers and software for any purpose. Mothers, especially, were rejectors from the start. Even more important, children, overall, wanted to use computers for gaming, not for education.

While some analysts view resistance as a deep-seated personality trait, others assume that it is a natural and ubiquitous human condition. Alcorn (1986, p. 32), for example, argues that humanity "has the survival trait of homeostasis, that is, a *natural resistance to change*" (emphasis ours).

Another, more sociologically-based perspective begins with people and the statuses (positions) they hold at the time of the innovation. This status-related perspective connects receptivity to people's perceptions of the impact on them if the innovation were to be adopted and carried out. When an innovation is perceived by people as leading to strong benefits such as more security, a better role image, less toil, more authority or power or salary, then they are more likely, personality differences aside, to be receptive to that innovation. The opposite is true when people view an innovation as posing serious uncertainties, threats, or risks (Giacquinta, 1975a, 1975b; Cancian, 1967; Katz, 1992; Kazlow, 1974, 1977; Lane, 1993; Ramos, 1980; Yarcheski and Mahon 1985, 1986). Perceptions of status-related risks and benefits appear to have played a part in why parents and children were mostly unreceptive to the idea of using home computers for educational purposes.

As noted in earlier chapters, parents knew little about academic software and academic computing; they seemed to fear the worst about these unknowns. Many believed that their children would not benefit from such software and computing since they saw these forms of software and computing to be "for those with learning disabilities" or "those behind in their achievement." Most felt that their children were doing well enough at school. Therefore, it would be of no benefit – indeed, it would be a waste of valuable energy, money, and time – to engage in such computer efforts at home. Other parents feared that the time required from them to make their homes places of computerized learning would be excessive. Parents worried that their support skills were not good enough. Some appeared to believe that if they insisted on educational computing at home, their children would have problems at school; such an effort would be seen as a challenge to the school's "educational authority." Others saw the cost of continually upgrading software – in the few cases where they actually believed effective software to exist – as too high. And finally, many who avoided the computer felt that their authority, while at the computer, would be undermined. All of this may have been tied to a general fear that they would be assuming the heavy responsibility of instruction if their children were to begin using their home computers seriously for education. In short, parents seemed to associate the possibility of "educational empowerment" with unacceptable risks rather than with desirable benefits.

Children, too, were opposed to the use of educational software and their home computers in the learning of academics, especially in the learning of academics apart from what the school dictated. Coming home to yet more work, as dictated by their parents, was not appealing to them. While some parents and children did see the value of the computer for word processing papers, this use of the machine simply replaced the typewriter. In some ways it was easier to do papers (a benefit) once they overcame the start-up time for buying and then learning how to use the word processing program.

Skill. Not only were most parents and children unreceptive to the use of educational software, but they also lacked the skills necessary to utilize it fully. Educational software, as we discussed earlier, is seldom self-explanatory. It can be frustrating to use, at least initially. But there is more to the matter of skill.

Frequently, innovations require fundamental changes in outlook and behavior. Many of these changes simply cannot be made unless potential implementers go through resocialization – a process of change – with some assistance. This means jettisoning old habits and beliefs and acquiring new ones. The expense in time, money, and energy is often great, so great that they are not available in the quantity and quality necessary to see the resocialization process through. The lack of parental and child skills for using educational software has been mentioned in various parts of this book. The help needed to resocialize the family members in our study, even if they were willing to engage in such a process, simply was not there for them.

Understanding. Yet a third personal characteristic strongly affects use or implementation. Even if people are willing to make changes, and even if the time, resources, and energy to make them are present, people often do not understand what personal changes in outlook and behavior are necessary in order to effectively carry out the proposed innovation. Moreover, an innovation's purposes and procedures are all too often outlined in brochures, booklets, or brief presentations. However, clarity and understanding seldom come in this way. In Chapter 9, we explained that promulgators of educational computing need to provide clear, understandable images of ways children and parents can best engage in educational computing at home. They might take the alternate strategy of helping families develop such images. Without a vision of what to do, however one comes by it, adequate implementation will not happen.

COMPATIBILITY OF THE EXISTING SOCIAL ENVELOPE

Although implementer characteristics are important, so are the properties of the existing social setting or envelope. Central to an innovation's effective use is the compatibility of the surrounding social (organizational) envelope. If the social demands or expectations pressing on individuals are incompatible with the purposes and procedures inherent in the innovation, it is much less likely to be implemented. Herein lies one reason why, as we have noted elsewhere in the book, innovations and especially new technologies are used, in the beginning, in ways that are least disruptive to the existing setting.

Families made the home computer compatible with their *existing* social envelope by accepting it largely as a game machine for children or as a sophisticated typewriter. Both uses fit nicely into preexisting family structures, in which school papers were typed at home and children had become used to playing Atari or Intellivision.[7] If the computer was to be used for anything else, parents expected the school, as was customary, to determine this. The school chose to emphasize programming and computer literacy. To push parents into the center of *academic* learning through the use of computers and educational software would have required *major* changes in the envelopes surrounding middle- and upper-middle-class families and in the relations between families and schools. We will have more to say about home–school relations in Chapter 11.

PRESENCE OF NECESSARY MATERIAL RESOURCES

Material resources are another prerequisite for social change. No matter how knowledgeable, willing, and able they are, people will be unable to implement even clearly articulated innovations – especially technological ones – without the necessary material resources. For example, discussion abounds about schools using computer-based, computer-integrated, or computer-assisted instruction. Each of these concepts requires a level of technology that, up to now, has been present in few institutions, even where teachers and administrators appear "revved up to go." In most of the families we studied, the number of educational software programs was so small that little serious educational computing would have been possible even if many of the other facilitating conditions had been present. In addition, as noted in Chapter 4, a good deal of the educational software on the market could not be used on some of the home computers.

PREVAILING CHANGE STRATEGIES

More has been written about the strategies employed by planners and agents of change than perhaps any other topic in the literature on planned organizational change. Three such strategies can be discerned in the literature: top-down or mandated strategies, bottom-up or grass roots strategies, and collaborative or participatory strategies.[8]

Current thinking is that the more participatory the strategy for change, the more effective the quality of the innovation as well as its implementation. As many professional change agents today argue, a change strategy that involves the participation of all interested parties in the decision-making process surrounding an innovative effort is the surest way of gaining individual cooperation, ownership, and receptivity to an innovation. "Power sharing" and "power equalization" are other terms used to refer to participation in fostering receptivity, overcoming resistance, or avoiding the emergence of resistance. Change agents believe that the surest way to undermine the successful implementation of an innovation is to mandate it from the top.

At the macro or national level, strategies for promoting educational computing at home, if they are to be called strategies, have been implemented from the top down. Change messages are sent one way – from hardware and software creators to families through promotional pieces or advertisements in magazines, newspapers, and TV and through computer vendors. While companies and proponents obviously have no authority or power to impose or mandate innovations, they urge parents to buy and to use computers and software for educational purposes.

At the micro or home level, change strategies are more varied. In some of the families we studied, parents and children collaborated on decisions concerning the adoption and use of the home computer. In others, the children lobbied for a computer – a kind of bottom-up strategy. Most often, however, computers and proposed *educational* uses were handed from parents to children in a top-down manner. It should come as no surprise, therefore, that in families where parents tried to pressure children into using the home computer for educational purposes, many children resisted even more.

The prevailing views about effective strategies of change suggest they must have yet another important feature: the presence, encouragement, and assistance of experts such as professional change agents. No current national strategy for home educational computing seems to exhibit this feature. Families, on their own, may seek and get some advice from computer salespeople. But merchandisers are not experts in the professional change-agent sense, and their principal motive is to get families to *buy* hardware and software. Parents may also try to get direction from the few knowledgeable school people who may be present. External change agents were present in several experimental efforts, which we discuss in Chapter 11, where computer and software companies and selected public school districts, in collaboration, sent computers and software home with children.

Current thinking about effective tactics of change also emphasizes the need for local advocacy, even when an outside change expert is present. Certainly, nearly all of the families we studied had not become academically empowered, in part because most parents did not want to assume a leadership or advocacy role in promoting the use of their home computers for academics. The need for strategies that ensure local leadership – a local member's "pressure and support" (see Huberman and Miles, 1984) – remains critical.

Finally, the current literature strongly suggests that a successful change strategy must promote everyday resocialization efforts and feedback. Many, if not most, potential implementers need substantial and continued help in developing and maintaining a clear vision, willingness, and skill.

When strategies do not ensure such help over time, potential users are unlikely to make difficult changes. As Fullan (1991, p. 96) explains, change strategies are needed to help potential users overcome the daily difficulties that arise in trying something new:

> One of the basic reasons why planning fails is that planners or decision-makers of change are unaware of the situations that potential implementers are facing. They introduce changes without providing a means to identify and confront the situational constraints and without attempting to understand the values, ideas, and experiences of those who are essential for implementing any changes.

Drawing on the work of Lippitt, Miles, and other planned change scholars and researchers, Fullan (1991, p. 222) summarizes the roles of internal and external change agents. One group of external consultants working on an ambitious school project, he points out, made "school people aware of new practices." Obviously this is an effective method of diffusion. They also helped schools "choose among a range of alternatives that matched local needs." In other words, they fostered the adoption process. Finally, these external facilitators – as they were called – involved themselves in a variety of other activities meant to facilitate implementation: they arranged for and conducted training (resocialization); ensured that resources and facilities would be available; and helped plan implementation and continuation support.

Clearly, the above change activities of outside facilitators would have benefited the families in our study. Given the nature of the prevailing strategies used by promoters of home educational computing, such activities were not possible.

CLOSING THE GAPS IN THE CHANGE PROCESS

Creators and champions of home educational computing need to examine more critically the change strategies they currently employ or endorse. At present, most of these are little more than long-distance, piecemeal, and truncated strategies; each focuses on the diffusion of particular pieces of hardware or particular pieces of software, with little or no regard for the others, or for what happens once these pieces are bought by families. Moreover, the objective of these strategies is primarily to convey images – in the marketplace through print and electronic media – of home educational computing as easy and fun.

The marketing images of happy, eager parents and children using computers and software in a problem-free atmosphere may promote good feelings, but they belie the actual reality. These simple happy "buy it and do it" portrayals gloss over

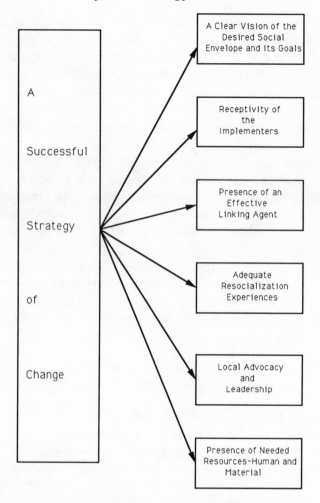

Figure 10.1. Components of a successful strategy of change.

the conditions needed for informed and sound adoption and for adequate implementation. They obscure the pressing need to develop strategies that foster such change desiderata as clear visions, receptivity, the presence of local leadership, adequate resocialization experiences, and the presence of necessary material resources (Figure 10.1).

In sum, to create the conditions necessary for effective diffusion, adoption, and ultimately, implementation of home educational computing, advocates of educational computing at home need to deal with families "up close" – to borrow a phrase from Huberman and Miles (1984). Our analysis suggests that in order to get close to children and their parents, those advocates will have to overcome their largely long-distance, piecemeal, truncated strategies of change. One way for creators and advocates to get closer – to erase or avoid these gaps – is to work through the schools as local facilitators. But as we discuss in Chapter 11, schools cannot become effective linking agents without a great deal of further thought and change.

NOTES

1. To reiterate a key point of Chapter 9: changing the social envelope at home for the educational computing of children would mean proposing changes in (1) the attitudes about computers and behaviors of parents and children at the computer, (2) the ways they relate to each other (their patterns of interaction) around the computer, and (3) aspects of the larger family environment. In other words, to change the home's social envelope it will be necessary to change aspects of family culture and social structure.

   It is also important to reiterate that there is no *one* appropriate social envelope for educational computing. The shape of an effective envelope depends upon many factors, including the number and nature of the family members as well as the *kind* of educational computing desired. The proposed social envelope for, say, math learning could be very different at least in some ways from that for learning how to write. Of course, certain new social expectations, behaviors, or relations might transcend specific purposes.

2. Over the years, scholars and researchers have tried to answer a number of fundamental questions about planned change, especially in education. These questions revolve around the "stages" that seem to comprise the process of planned organizational change: research and development, diffusion, adoption, implementation, and long-term implementation (often called institutionalization or incorporation).

One central question has to do with the development of an innovation and the reasons behind its creation. Some scholars have explored the kinds of problems or dissatisfactions that prompt the creation of innovations and have tried to determine who does the creating. Others have investigated how advocates of innovations emerge and become associated with specific planned changes.

A second important question deals with diffusion or initiation. Once created, what influences the spread of an innovation or knowledge about an innovation within a population of potential users, be they individuals or groups? Why do some potential users know about the innovation and others not? Some have also asked why and how innovations are initiated in local settings. Here, researchers have tried to uncover differences in the ways that social units such as schools isolate a difficulty or dissatisfaction and then consider various solutions (innovations).

A third key question has to do with adoption. Why do some potential users decide to try an innovation, while others do not? The emphasis is on the decision to try an innovation, not on the subsequent trying itself. The literature strongly suggests that many individuals and organizations decide to try innovations without subsequently ever acting upon their decisions. It also makes painfully clear that the adoption of an innovation does not guarantee the quality or quantity of its use.

Still a fourth critical question deals with implementation. Once an adopted innovation is introduced into a local setting, to what extent is it enacted properly? That is to say, to what extent are needed role changes carried out? The literature strongly supports the conclusion that in settings where efforts are made to implement an innovation, frequently the result is distortion and maladaptation, as opposed to the desired enactment or healthy adaptation.

Finally, there is a fifth question, which has to do with sustained use. Even though an innovation is being effectively implemented in a particular setting, other conditions must be met or avoided in order to ensure that it will endure, that it will become institutionalized. If relatively few innovations are satisfactorily implemented, still fewer ever reach incorporation. We do not consider institutionalization in our study because it was too early to expect to find it in the homes we examined.

Each of these issues should be regarded as distinct aspects of the overall question of how to arrive at effective tactics of change.

164

Yet, many change promoters and some past students of change have not differentiated between diffusion and adoption or among diffusion, adoption, and implementation.

3. The problem of diffusing and of promoting the adoption of educational computing at home (or at school) is complex because these two processes occur through the diffusion and adoption of specific pieces of educational software and specific pieces of hardware. Considering that there are literally thousands of pieces of software and hundreds of pieces of computer-related hardware, their diffusion and adoption can occur at dramatically different rates and in dramatically different ways. Thus, the global diffusion and adoption of educational computing is far from a simple matter.

4. At the time of this writing, it is estimated that nearly 24 million homes (Stacey, 1991) have personal computers; another estimate is that about one out of four students goes home to personal computers (Lewis, 1992).

5. Obviously, most innovations are not adopted by everyone. Indeed, the majority of people probably never adopt many innovations. And, even when some adopt and then use an innovation, they may discontinue its use at some point – early or late.

   Rogers discusses many characteristics that seem to predispose people to adopt early, late, or never. Two fundamental factors of early adoption, which were reflected in our study of home computers, were (1) the potential adopter's socioeconomic status and (2) the extent to which he or she was cosmopolitan or local in outlook and access to knowledge. The more cosmopolitan an individual (in the sense of social location), the more likely it is that he or she will know about a promising innovation; the higher one's socioeconomic status (which determines affordability), the more likely one is to adopt an innovation and to do so earlier. The families in our study were by and large from the middle to upper-middle class and in one way or another were cosmopolitan enough to have obtained knowledge or information about computers. These trends did not hold for the matter of educational software.

6. For other important conceptual and empirical differences between the individual adopter and the organizational implementation perspectives, see the discussions of Gross, Giacquinta, and Bernstein (1971, pp. 19–39) and of Rogers (1983, pp. 87–133).

7. The school emphasized programming and computer literacy for the same reasons that parents allowed gaming and word process-

ing; these were the least disruptive uses of the machines. Both of these could be confined mainly to labs where one or two teachers who had some interest or skill could teach programming and computer literacy in the same way that all other subjects were taught. Computers used in this manner would fit into the existing curriculum and daily routine of the school with little or no disruption. Classroom instruction accurately classified as computer-based or computer-integrated or even computer-assisted represents a grave disruption to the existing social envelope. This magnitude of innovation would have been – and still is – met with strong resistance from teachers and administrators.

8. For more recent discussions with useful overviews on this topic, see Cross (1984), Kanter (1983), Huberman and Miles (1984), and Loucks-Horsley and Hergert (1985).

Chapter 11

Reexamining the Home–School Computer Connection

If appropriate uses of microcomputers in the home are to further educational opportunities, there must be clear and coordinated instructional goals that are developed and accepted by both parents and teachers. (Kinzer and others, 1985, p. 122)

In Chapter 10, we argued that the "long-distance" change strategies of many creators account in part for the limited diffusion and adoption of educational software and, even more important, for the minimal implementation of such software once adopted by families. As highlighted earlier, most families in our study had little awareness of, interest in, or accurate information about good educational software or how to use it effectively once they had it. The schools their children attended did not or could not offer much assistance in this regard. Families that were interested seemed at a loss about where to go to get such information and help. A third broad lesson of our research is that much greater effort needs to be devoted to creating and maintaining effective linking agents to families.

In this chapter, we examine the viability of schools as effective linking agents for home academic computing.[1] After discussing home–school relations in general, we focus on home–school relations surrounding the computer, noting some of the collaborations under way around the country that are promoting educational computing both in school and at home. Then we consider some important conditions that need to be addressed if schools are to become effective links. We also consider several other possible links.

THE SCHOOL AS AN EFFECTIVE
LINKING AGENT

Is the school currently an effective mechanism for informing families about educational software and hardware and for fostering their use at home for academic computing? Part of the answer depends on the general state of home–school relations today. Part depends on their specific state of relations regarding computers.

THE HOME–SCHOOL CONNECTION IN
GENERAL

A great deal of recent educational literature has been devoted to the importance of *strengthening* home–school relations through greater parental involvement (e.g., Crowson, 1992; Driscoll, 1992; Epstein, 1986, 1987, 1989, 1991; Fullan, 1991; Henderson, 1988; Olson, 1990; Swap, 1991).

A good part of this involvement, it is argued, needs to occur in the home, with parents taking a more direct and active part in their children's homework and education in general. As the 1987 Metropolitan Life Survey underscores, the majority of teachers and parents believe that many or most parents "fail to motivate [children] to learn, take too little interest in their children's education in general, and neglect to see that their children's homework gets done" (Olson, 1990, p. 17).

In addition to educational activities at home, the concept of parent involvement includes contact with and participation at school: parents communicating with their children's teachers and with the school as a whole; parents observing and volunteering for instructional and noninstructional school activities; parents taking part in school and school-related community decision making and other activities (Epstein, 1989; Fullan, 1991). Parental involvement in these activities is extremely low.

Educators say, however, that children show higher achievement in school, have better attitudes about school, and are more likely to behave better in school when their parents are involved. Students who have not been performing well academically are likely to do better when their parents are asked to help. When children see that their parents care about education, take an interest in education, and hold high expectations for success in school, they are more likely to value education themselves and therefore to strive to achieve in school (Jennings, 1990).

It is best for children when both home and school reinforce the same values and expectations and when parents and teachers act jointly to achieve their goals. As the New Compact for Learning (*A New Compact for Learning*, 1991, p. 7), launched in New York State, points out:

> If children are to succeed in school, home and school must work together. When the school reflects the values of the home and the home supports the efforts of the school, children grow in an atmosphere of shared purpose and consistent expectations.

In spite of the research documenting the importance of compatible home and school relations, and in spite of reports that some schools are attempting to promote such relations, the typical connection between home and school remains weak.[2] As Olson (1990, p. 17) notes: "As the two major forces entrusted with educating and socializing children in society, parents and teachers should be natural allies. But far too often, they find themselves on opposite sides of an exceedingly high fence."

The results of the National Educational Longitudinal Survey of 1988 show that parents are cut off from the schools (Bacon, 1990). And, although it is now recognized that the home–school connection is important for junior and senior high school students, when there is a relationship, it is more likely to be with elementary schools. In testimony before the U.S. House of Representatives' Subcommittee on Select Education, Epstein (1989, p. 3) indicated that teacher practices of informing and involving parents "decline dramatically after the early elementary grades."

There are several explanations for the lack of connection between home and school. On one hand, teachers may fear parental interference, worry about whether parents are capable of helping their children educationally, or lack the time or the training to involve themselves in helping parents learn relevant skills.

Parents, on the other hand, may keep away from the school in part because they "do not understand middle and high school programs," or "teachers' expectations and requirements," or "early and later adolescent development" and "the learning, social, and personal problems their children face" (Epstein, 1989, pp. 3–4). In addition, parents may lack the time and the energy to work with their children at home or to involve themselves at school because they are working full-time, as is so often the case in both two-parent and single-parent households today. Simply put, it seems improbable that schools can be effective linking agents for home academic computing without important changes in the ways schools relate to families in general. Is the picture regarding their relationship in the area of educational computing any better?

THE HOME–SCHOOL CONNECTION
REGARDING EDUCATIONAL COMPUTING

At the time of the SITE study, educators had already begun suggesting that schools must make the effort to involve parents in children's educational computer activities. Epstein (1985, p. 31), for example, recommended:

> Just as schools expect parents to know about their children's textbooks, worksheets, and workbooks, schools must provide information to parents about the new learning materials that are becoming part of the school's instructional program, and this information can be extended to cover applications on home computers.

However, our research indicates that although some children were engaged in forms of educational computing at school – primarily programming – schools did not work with parents to promote these activities at home. Since very few, if any, of the schools involved students in academic computing, school-to-home contact about this kind of home computing was even less evident.

These findings have been echoed by other researchers. In the Second National Survey of Instructional Uses of School Computers (1986, Issue 3), Becker detected little increase in teacher–parent communication about computers. In a study of computers in early childhood education, Edyburn and Lartz (1986) found that most of the teachers surveyed had not been contacted by parents with questions about computers and, in addition, thought that they would not be able to answer such questions. Epstein (1985) noted that although schools should consider carefully how home computers might contribute to learning, few of them had tried to coordinate such activities. She explained how home computers could be used to provide activities for enrichment, remedial work, improving basic skills as well as thinking skills, writing, and computer literacy.

Home–school relations in educational computing have been no better. Indeed, for many reasons they appear worse. Since very few schools have actually integrated computers into their curricula, there is less reason for teachers to involve parents in such activities at home. Many teachers have resisted and continue to resist serious classroom use of computers for instruction.

The lack of necessary computer skills, motivation, and understanding among teachers is compounded by the enormity of the educational software field, limited budgets for the purchase of pieces thought to be good, and the difficulty and time-consuming task of learning about and effectively using such programs. Furthermore, teachers receive neither the training to develop their own competencies nor guidance in how to involve parents in their children's educational computing at home. Moreover, since the large majority of children do not have computers at home, teachers continue to feel that to involve only those parents with home computers is unfair.

SOME NOTEWORTHY HOME–SCHOOL EXCEPTIONS

This is not to say that hardware and software creators and others have made no effort to get teachers to integrate computers into their classroom curricula and to link school computer use with children's educational uses at home.[3] Apple, for example, launched its Apple Classroom of Tomorrow (ACOT) project in 1985 in five school sites around the country.[4] ACOT's goals were "to develop high access to technology in schools and homes, to support teachers through training, and to conduct studies in these learning contexts" (*Apple Classroom of Tomorrow*, 1989, p. 7).

The Indiana Buddy System Project is another example of home–school involvement. This is a statewide endeavor that now includes fourth-, fifth-, and sixth-graders in twenty schools who are also given computers, modems, and printers to use at home (Bruder, 1992, p. 16). The project objectives are to improve the creative writing skills of children, allow them to use telecommunications to extend their knowledge of the world and to develop research skills, and improve relations among parents, children, and teachers (Summers, Bertsch, and Smith, 1989). The teachers integrate computer use into the curriculum and conduct workshops to familiarize parents with computers. Summers and her associates (1989, p. 41) report that the "computer-in-the-home became an extension of the classroom."

Other school systems have initiated computer loan programs for families. For example, New York City, which has had a computer loan program in a few schools for several years, has introduced a new program, Project Tell, to motivate at-risk students to stay in school. The project places computers, printers, and modems in the homes of students at one elementary school and four intermediate schools ("Technology Links Classroom and Home," 1991).

The Houston School System, a pioneer in this area, allows its parents to borrow computers and software for periods of time, once they have received preliminary training. In addition, parents can purchase computers through a school discount program and those who have purchased computers though the program are permitted to borrow educational software from a lending library (Epstein, 1985).

Other school systems – including those in Buffalo, Detroit, Houston, New Mexico, and San Francisco – are also establishing programs to encourage parents to use educational software at home (D'Angelo & Adler, 1991; November, 1992; Ragsdale, 1988). Some systems are collaborating with Prescription Learning Corporation, creator of the Take-Home Computer Program, available in Apple IIe or MS-DOS format, which provides instructional courseware according to children's individual needs. Before computers are taken home, parent–student workshops are conducted to review the reading, mathematics, and writing software prescribed for a child. The general objectives of this program are to increase parental involvement, improve children's basic skills, develop their computer literacy, and provide them with more "time on task" (Prescription Learning, n.d.).

Although these attempts may be promising as models for fostering home educational computing via the schools, they represent a very small number of schools and families.[5] Nevertheless, such projects can provide a considerable amount of information about the conditions in families and in schools that would help schools become effective linking agents for educational computing at home.

The task for parents, schools, creators, and advocates of educational technology seems even greater when it is regarded as the implementation of a profound technological innovation. As linking agents, what would schools need to do to help parents and children implement this innovation? And, before they can help them do this, how would schools themselves need to change?

AS EFFECTIVE LINKS, HOW SCHOOLS WOULD NEED TO HELP FAMILIES

As effective linking agents, schools would have to help families establish clear and convincing visions of the social envelope needed at home in order to promote effective educational uses of computers. In addition, schools would need to help families cope with the processes of diffusion, adoption, and implementation of educational hardware and software in conformity with this home vision.

Most families have little or no sense of the social innovation behind their hardware and software. While some parts of a

Beyond Technology's Promise

new home envelope might be similar for many families, other parts might be individualized. These new images would be quite different from those that typically surround game playing in the home, but not entirely so in that children can also enjoy, experiment, and constructively play in the context of learning. Schools would need to guide parents and children in thinking about the various layers of the home envelope: their behavior at the computer, interaction around the computer, and involvement within the greater social context, including the school.

It takes time and energy – which many parents feel they do not have – to learn how to use a computer and to feel comfortable enough with one to assist others. And even if parents are computer-knowledgeable and even if they can program or use applications programs, this does not mean that they know about educational uses or are aware of the good educational programs and how to integrate them with schoolwork. Schools would, therefore, need to assist parents in learning about computers and about the educational uses of computers.

Since there is a vast, often overwhelming storehouse of information on computers and educational software, schools would have to facilitate the family's gathering of accurate and useful information about computers and their educational uses. Then they would need to help families make appropriate choices among the many potentially useful, but different, educational software packages and the various educational uses of tool software.

Schools would have to help children and parents become more interested in and more positive toward the educational uses of computers. One of their first tasks would be to persuade parents, especially mothers, to become involved with computers. Schools would also have to encourage parents to develop the skills and confidence required to help their children learn with computers.

In short, if schools are to become adequate linking agents, they will need to help families develop clear innovative visions, become more receptive to home educational computing, acquire adequate resocialization experiences that would lead to effective parental training and computer use, and locate information about educational computing and even some of the actual material and human resources needed. Also, schools would have to act as local advocates for academic computing and attempt to provide collaborative leadership with families during their implementation efforts. Although some educators think that computers can empower parents to take control of their children's education, our research suggests that most parents will not or cannot do so on their own. As underscored in Chapters 9 and 10, technological change of this kind is a complex and difficult process, and parents need help if they are to understand and cope with it.

TO HELP FAMILIES, WHAT MUST HAPPEN TO SCHOOLS?

The above is a tall order for an already beleaguered institution. While some schools, as previously discussed, do seem able to act (with outside help) as effective links for home computing, most do not have this capability at present. What would have to happen to these schools before they could help families?

Most schools continue to find it difficult to infuse computer use into their own classrooms (Becker, 1985, 1986, 1987, 1991; Levin, 1990; Watkins and Brimm, 1985). Therefore, a first step for them would be to develop a vision of effective computer use within their *own* classroom walls and a plan of action that takes into account the factors affecting the implementation of such a vision. In many cases, administrators and teachers have not recognized educational computing as a social innovation requiring the presence of certain conditions for successful implementation. Among other things, schools would have to make organizational and physical changes, provide initial and ongoing resources and training to teachers, and ensure continued administrative support. It is only then that they would be able to develop a plan for guiding parents.

Teachers have many responsibilities as it is. Asking them to help parents with computers is asking them to enact yet another and difficult innovation. A critical step would be to overcome the resistance of many teachers and make them more receptive to computers. In addition, teachers need to learn about the effective educational uses of computers and how to implement these uses in their classrooms. They also need to learn how to help parents develop computer competencies and create home environments that promote educational computing. In other words, they must be given the time and opportunity to gain the knowledge and to develop their own skills as well as the time to meet and work with parents.

Schools, like families, need linking agents. Administrators need to consider hiring change agents who specialize in computers in education and who could help school personnel see how to use computers for teaching effectively and how to make the necessary social and technological changes. Such experts could also help develop plans for parent involvement in school-related uses of computers at home. Such plans would foster communication between parents and schools about educational computing as well. Having such change agents would reduce the burden on teachers as well as provide them with needed encouragement and assistance.

The changes needed and the work necessary may seem daunting, especially now that school budgets are being cut. It will not be easy for teachers to motivate children to engage in educational computing at home or to motivate parents to become involved in their children's educational computer use. It will also not be easy for schools to help parents understand what they need to do, let alone foster their willingness and capabilities. It will take time, especially with computer illiterate and computer-phobic parents. However, schools need not try to do everything at once. They might start with what families now have instead of worrying about what they do not have. As Desai (1992, p. 20) pointed out recently for a non-school context:

> It is tempting to think that knowledge of the old order is irrelevant. But that is not correct. Even when you know where you want to go, you should know where you are coming from. The starting point constrains where you can go, how fast and in what precise way.

In summary, before schools can become effective linking agents, it will be necessary to help them undergo substantial structural changes, including the real integration of computers into classrooms. There needs to be a lot more deliberate thinking about the social envelopes of the school and of the home, and about the order and timing of change activities. As difficult as this transition may be, it seems unlikely that most schools will become adequate linking agents without such changes.

ALTERNATIVE LINKING AGENTS

The discussion above assumes that the home–school relationship is already compatible or can be made more so. As Epstein (1991, p. 349) has put it:

> Sometimes educators feel that it is simply impossible to jump the hurdles, remove the barriers, and solve the real problems that prevent them from viewing families as resources for promoting children's learning. . . . This view is too pessimistic. Shared vision and concerted effort have led to a variety of successful programs to connect schools, families, and communities. There is no excuse for not taking the first sure steps down one of the many paths to partnership.

Epstein does acknowledge, however, that some people do view the home and school as essentially incompatible. One, for instance, is Pournelle (1986, p. 23). In reflecting on how computers could revolutionize the way children are educated, he has argued:

> The educational establishment is never going to permit any fundamental reform of the school system. . . . What educationists can't do is prevent parents from teaching their kids to read and from sitting them down in front of a vast store of easily available information.

Those with this view of school and home relations would not be likely to consider the school a desirable linking agent.[6]

Another potential linking agent might take the form of a home educational extension service. It might be modeled after the U.S. Agricultural Extension Service, which promotes the diffusion, adoption, and utilization of new technologies among farmers and among nonfarmers through an expanded food and nutrition program. As a linking agent, the Agricultural Extension Service is one of the most ambitious and successful models in existence. Operating with federal, state, and local funds, its history dates back more than a century. According to Rogers (1988), the Extension Service currently employs about 17,000 professionals and 10,000 paraprofessional aides. It also uses several hundred thousand volunteers. The Extension Service has the capability of guiding research that meets users' needs and a system for diffusing research-based knowledge and information to farmers and for helping them to utilize it.[7]

The possibility for a parallel educational extension service involving families and educational technologies, especially computer-based, seems clear.[8] An educational extension service could get close to families in order to focus on their needs and could help direct and integrate university research to meet these needs. National in scope and local in application, it could emphasize the diffusion of hardware and software innovations to families and provide the guidance families would need to use them.

A second alternative to the school as a linking agent might be called a consortium for home educational technologies. It could be modeled after the private, nonprofit Alliance for Technology Access, a federation of forty-six consultation centers across the nation. By providing information, technical support, and demonstrations and by lending equipment and software, these centers help families with disabled children increase their access to modern technology.[9]

By focusing on the needs of mainstream families at various income levels, such a consortium for home educational technologies could be broader in scope than the more specialized consortium for the disabled. A consortium might not have the interest in or capacity to direct research in the same way that an extension service might, but it might be able to get even closer to families and might not necessarily be in competition with schools as much as a complement to them. One such promising effort that is now being launched is EPIE Institute's Let Our Children Learn Project. The project is being designed to work directly with families on home educational computing independently of the schools.[10]

A full discussion of the pros and cons of these two alternatives or other possible linking agents would take us far afield of our present topic.[11] It should be pointed out, however, that the tasks of providing clear home visions, adequate socialization experiences, implementation support, local leadership, and collaboration apply to these alternatives as much as they do to schools.[12]

Our intent in this chapter has been to underscore the crucial need for effective linking agents. We asked whether at present most schools could act as effective linking agents for families and offered some possible alternatives. None that we have discussed, however, would make the job of connecting families and effective software and hardware any easier. In Chapter 12, we review our basic findings and the three broad lessons derived from them. To illustrate their importance for other educational technologies, we apply these lessons to arguably the most promising new technology: educational multimedia.

NOTES

1. Hardware and software creators may see the *school,* not the family, as their direct client. Given this frame of mind, the object of their change strategies would be the school: its teachers and its students. Academic and other forms of educational computing *may* spill over into homes with computers, but these are "artifacts" of school activities. It is also possible that creators are interested in promoting children's computing at home but think that this *will happen naturally* as children use computers and software at school. In either case, those who focus on the school may feel that the issue of treating the school as a linking agent

for the home is irrelevant. However, we believe that the issues of home–school relations and of linking agents have relevance even for those who choose to focus on the school, since what happens in school is strongly affected by parent and child actions or inaction at home.

Another matter relevant to making the home the focal point of interest is the availability of computers to families. A large majority of families with children still do not have home computers and many, especially those at the lower ends of the economic ladder, probably cannot afford to buy them without seriously altering family priorities. Without computers at home, it may seem odd to be discussing the use of the school or any other entity as a linking agent. The point is that a child has more opportunity, more time, to use a computer at home than in school. So the home might very well be more important, or at least as important as the school, as the main point of interest.

2. Some schools have worked at creating and maintaining various ways of keeping parents informed. They send reports and newsletters home, schedule parent–teacher conferences, maintain voice hotlines, invite parents to class functions, create parent resource centers in school, hold workshops to teach parents specific techniques for helping their children learn, encourage parents to volunteer, make home visits, produce videotapes that demonstrate techniques parents can use, and sponsor radio programs that encourage parent participation (see, e.g., D'Angelo and Adler, 1991; Olson, 1990; Swap, 1991). In addition, some schools have tried to make parents part of the school by involving them in school decisions. Partnerships in which parents are informed about and become involved in their children's education and in school activities are beginning to be supported at the national, state, district, and local school levels. For a discussion of such efforts see the collection of papers in *Phi Delta Kappan*, vol. 72, no. 5 (January 1991), pp. 345–88.

3. Of course, schools may choose to, and sometimes do, act on their own as the conduit for home use or as the sole impetus for the educational computing of children. They become the promoter and change agent, and in this regard are already much closer to the clients of diffusion and implementation: the parents and their children. If these schools can get software and hardware creators to help them, rather than the other way around, then such grass roots strategies might possibly be more successful

than the top-down approaches of promoters and creators. Nevertheless, one still needs to be mindful that many of the obstacles that get in the way of the more distant creators and promoters may also prevail when someone or some group locally decides that the school will become the conduit for educational computing at home.

4. The school systems were located in Blue Earth, Minnesota; Columbus, Ohio; Cupertino, California; Eugene, Oregon; and, Memphis, Tennessee. One class in each of these school systems was chosen, with Apple lending each student an Apple IIe at school and a IIc at home (the ninth-grade class in Columbus got Macintoshes). Modems at home permitted children to communicate with tutors. Apple provided a coordinator and training workshops for teachers on the hardware and software supplied by over thirteen third-party developers (Shalvoy, 1987b, p. 19). Ross and others (1990, p. 5) report that the 1985–7 school years show ACOT classes to be superior to non-ACOT classes in basic skills, grade-equivalent gain scores, and attitudes toward learning and school activities. They note that the results from the 1987–8 program are less consistent or clear, but tend to favor ACOT students on standardized achievement subtests and attitude measures. In another follow-up assessment of ACOT, Baker, Gearhart, and Herman (1990, p. 8) report among other findings that "ACOT parents generally felt the project had benefited their children in their knowledge of computers, attitudes toward learning, and achievement, though they had some concerns about curriculum coverage."

5. Even if the effectiveness and quality of their implementation were to be firmly established, one must be careful about arriving at any conclusions. Similar innovative efforts in other educational areas have often succeeded as demonstrations, only to fail during widespread implementation.

6. The desire for an alternative linking agent, however, need not be based on the assumption that home and school are in conflict. Those who see the schools as compatible but also inadequate as a provider of these computer linking services might also search for an alternative connecting mechanism. This might be especially useful for families that have children at risk or with disabilities and that want to provide their children with educational support at home beyond those available at their schools.

7. Rogers (1988, pp. 505–6) outlines many characteristics of the Agricultural Extension Service: for example, it offers many

potentially useful innovations for clients and a research arm that focuses on client utilization; it provides a high degree of user contact and input, and a spannable social distance between each component in the technology transfer system; and it represents an effective self-contained system of research, development, diffusion, and utilization.

8. Whether schools could be clients or in some way be part of such an extension service remains to be explored. It is not clear that they need to be excluded.

9. In a first effort to determine how children are using computers at home for educational purposes and how the Alliance is helping, Adele Schwartz at Teachers College is proposing to study families with disabled children who belong to the Alliance. This proposed research was shared during several face-to-face meetings.

10. This information was shared by the executive director of the EPIE Institute, Ken Komoski, during a recent phone conversation with the senior author.

11. Examples of other linking agent options include community organizations such as libraries and museums and home educational computer groups, similar to the general computer-user groups currently found around the country.

12. It is quite possible that these mechanisms – the schools, an extension service, and a consortium – may be more complementary than their presentation here may suggest. Their feasibility, value, and relationship – as well as that of other possible linking mechanisms – deserve serious attention in the future.

Chapter 12

Where Do We Go from Here?

We need to spend more effort trying to understand the dynamics of technology as it evolves in different social contexts, and less time promoting or denouncing technology itself. (Garcia, 1991, p. 29)

We began our book by discussing the educational promise of the home computer. In this final chapter, we summarize briefly what our research unearthed about the current reality behind this promise and recap the lessons learned from our study of home educational computing. We then use the example of "interactive multimedia" to illustrate why creators, advocates, educators, and families will need to take these lessons to heart if they wish to get beyond the educational promise of *any* educational technology. We end with a discussion about the kinds of research needed in the future.

THE EDUCATIONAL PROMISE OF
THE HOME COMPUTER

The early and middle 1980s saw the publication of national reports critical of public schooling in the United States. The disenchantment was partly a response to the inadequate number of educated men and women in the work force. It was also triggered by the nation's failure to fulfill its goal of ensuring greater equality of educational opportunity and achievement for its children.

Searching for more effective ways to meet these needs, many reformers saw great promise in the home computer as a tutor and a tool for academic and other forms of learning. Some believed that computer use at home would help children do better at school, that they would be more motivated to learn, and would show increased achievement. Others added that the computer would empower parents to educate their children at home, apart from what happened at school.

THE REALITY: FALTERING PROMISES

Using qualitative research methods during the three-year period from early 1984 through 1986, we studied families in the greater New York tristate area. Our examination of the survey and market-research literature at that time indicated that little was yet known about the actual state of home educational computing. Moreover, the situation was being distorted by reports in the popular press based on atypical computer-using families.

Our in-depth investigation involved seventy families, demographically similar to those with children across the nation who were purchasing home computers. We found that very few children were using their home computers as tutors for the learning of academic subjects and as tools or tutees for other educational purposes, although there was some school-connected programming and word processing. However, the educational home efforts that we uncovered were for the most part sporadic. Our investigation led us, therefore, to the conclusion that the educational promise of the home computer was not being fulfilled. There is little reason to believe that the situation has changed.

Our study also led to the conclusion that a complex set of predominantly social factors has prevented parents from encouraging and assisting their children in educational computing activities. These factors are partly a function of their lack of awareness about useful educational software and of their perceptions about its high cost and low quality. Other reasons included their limited time, lack of interest in or skill with computers, fear of computers, and reliance on the schools for their children's learning agenda. Many parents seemed content in the widespread belief that exposure at home to a computer for *any* purpose gives children a real advantage at school and in the future. The children's schools did not integrate computers into their classrooms for instructional purposes. They taught about computers as another subject, holding classes in computer literacy and programming. And, reinforced by siblings and peers, children simply did not want to use their computers at home for serious educational computing, preferring to use them as game machines.

THE LESSONS LEARNED

Our study yielded three broad lessons: (1) that the changes needed in a home's social envelope when a computer is introduced must be more clearly defined and communicated to families; (2) that even if families are armed with a clear vision of these changes, most still need help in overcoming the barriers of software diffusion, adoption, and especially implementation; and (3) to be effective linking agents for this process of educational change at home, schools must undergo substantial changes themselves and in their relations with families.

These lessons need to be heeded if the quantity and quality of home educational computing are to improve. During our countless hours of thinking, discussing, and writing, we had many ideas about concrete activities that creators, linking agents (whether they be schools or other social entities), and families might try out in order to advance home educational computing. We present some of these thoughts in Appendix E.

But there is more. We believe that the above lessons apply to home-related educational technologies across the board. To demonstrate the *general* importance of these lessons, we use "interactive multimedia" as an example.[1] We begin with a description of this promising educational technology.

INTERACTIVE MULTIMEDIA:
A PROMISING NEW TECHNOLOGY

Interactive multimedia can be defined as "the combination of video, sound, text, animation, and graphics with a computer to tie these components together" ("Multimedia: How It Changes the Way We Teach and Learn," 1991, p. 22). One of the advantages of interactive multimedia is that it presents more complete information than any one medium alone can, that it accommodates children with different learning styles, and that its interactive quality stimulates children to be active, motivated learners (Char, 1985; Greenfield, 1985; "Multimedia," 1991; Kay, 1991; Kozma, 1991; Withrow, 1985).

Interactive multimedia often use videodiscs to store data. Videodiscs can hold 54,000 frames, accessible in any order. When a videodisc player is connected to a computer and monitor, the user is able to interact with the software. People working individually or in small groups can control such programs themselves to learn subject matter, explore environments, and design projects that contain text, illustrations, moving images, and sound. If a videodisc does not come with accompanying software, users can use *HyperCard* or similar hypertext programs such as *LinkWay* to design their projects.

One example of a videodisc multimedia program is *The '88 Vote: Campaign for the White House,* created by ABC News in conjunction with Optical Data Corporation.[2] In her review of *The '88 Vote,* Lehrer (1989, p. 18) writes that the program "combines video segments, photographs, computer graphics, and textual data-bases with HyperCard stacks." HyperCard stacks can be used to access the video and textual information in any way one chooses. Users can watch a speech and read the text at the same time, take notes, or use the "documentary maker" to customize videodisc segments, thus creating "their own presentations or multimedia reports based on just those parts of the video segments that are relevant."

Created at the Bank Street College of Education, *Palenque* is another example of an interactive videodisc program. With this program one can visit an archaeological site as a member of a research team "exploring ancient Maya ruins in search of the tomb of Pacal, the 12-year-old ruler of Palenque during its heyday" (Kozma, 1991, p. 200). The joystick permits one to move around the site. Simulated research tools include a camera, compass, and tape recorder. One can access information from a data base, question an archaeologist, read about Mayan hieroglyphics, or listen to jungle sounds (Berger, 1989; Char and Wilson, 1986; Kozma, 1991).[3]

While companies continue to create interactive multimedia programs with videodiscs, newer, compact-disk players promise even more. One advantage of this technology is that it stores data in digital form, allowing the user to manipulate data and to send it to other computers. CD-ROM (Compact Disk–Read Only Memory) educational disks are already available. Salpeter (1991, p. 35) describes several:

> There are now multimedia reference tools that present an entire encyclopedia on a single CD, complete with drawings or photos of images; realistic music and sound effects; and animated sequences to illustrate important concepts. Children can page through colorfully illustrated CD-ROM storybooks and hear words, phrases, or the entire story read aloud – in a choice of languages. And students of all ages can learn about music with the help of new CD-ROM applications that combine high-quality recordings with written commentary; animated scores; textual translations; glossaries that include examples the learner can listen to; and other illustrated lessons.

Salpeter describes CD-ROM based technologies especially relevant for homes, including CD-I (Compact Disk–Interactive players, intended as home entertainment systems) and CDTV (Commodore Dynamic Total Vision, also aimed at the home consumer).[4] Educational programs for both of these two technologies are now being developed (Salpeter, 1991, pp. 30–40).

Testimonials and observations about interactive multimedia make its *educational* promise seem unquestionable: "perhaps as important a milestone as Gutenberg's invention of the printing press" (McClain, 1983, p. 79); "the most powerful instructional tool I have ever discovered" (Howe, 1985, p. 8); "powerful new teaching tools unlike any you've seen before" (Brady, 1989, p. 56); "the rage in educational technology these days" (Salpeter, 1991, p. 33).

APPLICATION OF THE THREE LESSONS
TO INTERACTIVE MULTIMEDIA

While the current optimism about interactive multimedia reminds us of the enthusiasm that initially surrounded the simple computer and while we acknowledge that this technology "looks" educationally promising, we wonder how well it will fare in homes?[5] In comparison with "simple" educational computing, multimedia involves more, not less open-ended decision making and use; necessitates greater, not less computer and technology competence; requires more, not less equipment; and involves more not less expenditures of resources – money, time, and energy. We believe that the answer to the question as posed therefore depends on whether the lessons of our research can be taken to heart, that is, whether we can (1) articulate the needed changes in a home's social envelope; (2) ensure the presence of conditions that foster diffusion, adoption, and implementation; and (3) create and maintain effective home linking agents.

A VISION OF CHANGES IN THE
HOME ENVELOPE

In the case of home educational computing, creators and advocates have yet to deal effectively with the fact that hardware and software are being introduced into existing family systems that often minimize or adversely affect their educational use. Since little emphasis has been put on the needed home changes, families have had little or no vision of what needs changing or direction in this regard. It is unlikely that home multimedia will be used to any greater extent without such a vision. Families will need to understand the expectations at the hands-on, the social-interaction, and the social-ecological layers of the home envelope. Since multimedia programs are very complex and open-ended, it could be especially easy for parents and children to become overwhelmed and to founder without them.

ATTENTION TO DIFFUSION, ADOPTION, AND IMPLEMENTATION

The notion that it is only necessary to purchase machines and software and that they will "do the job on their own with children" has not worked so far; it will most likely not work with educational multimedia either. As in the case of "simple" educational home computing, the use of multimedia will need to be viewed as the result of a process of social change and a set of facilitators.

What is the likelihood that parents will buy multimedia equipment and software for their children's educational use at home? Because of the additional costs, it seems highly unlikely that such hardware and software will be adopted in the numbers that families adopted stand-alone computers, at least not without the effective diffusion of accurate knowledge about software, convincing evidence that it really can have the effects promised, and knowledge about what parents, children, and other social units have to do to make the promise come true.

As in the case of educational computing, it is reasonable to assume that children will need parental leadership and advocacy to implement educational multimedia effectively. This new computer-based technology will likely require open-ended, nonlinear thinking and the learning of higher-order concepts and thinking skills. It offers greater user control and random access of information. As laudable as these features are, their implementation will likely require considerable parental leadership in the form of coaching, modeling, and scaffolding. In addition, because of the increasing complexity of the hardware, a user will probably need considerable prerequisite knowledge or experience with a similar technology.

How likely is it that parents will be able or willing to assist their children with this challenging technology? Many of the factors that influenced the utilization of personal computers appear pertinent here as well. In addition to *understanding* the purposes and roles required for the utilization of multimedia hardware and software, other conditions need to be fostered: notably, family *receptivity* to and *advocacy* of multimedia educational use. These are affected in part by one's perceptions of the benefits and risks of multimedia use and one's user *skills*. It is quite likely that all of these could be enhanced if positive *training* (resocialization) and affordable *hardware and software* with *demonstrated* effectiveness were available.

CREATING EFFECTIVE LINKING AGENTS

In the case of straight academic computing, it was obvious that most families could not go it alone. They needed but did not get outside, up-close help in bringing about the necessary conditions for diffusion, adoption, and implementation, even when they were receptive to the notion of children's educational computing at home. However, because of conditions at most schools and because of the nature of home–school communication, schools have not been able to act as up-close linking agents. They have not been able to foster the conditions required for successful planned change mentioned in the preceding section. Unless an effort is made to help schools change, they will not become effective linking agents for children's multimedia uses at home either.

Perhaps the diffusion, adoption, and implementation might be bolstered through the creation of other linking agents (such as an extension service or a consortium of state and local organizations) or existing cultural institutions (such as libraries, museums, and zoos).

Although this section has focused on one new promising cluster of technological innovations – interactive multimedia – other kinds of promising educational technologies are available for the home, such as those built around telecommunications. Whatever the educational technology, the findings and the lessons presented in this book merit the serious attention of creators, advocates, researchers, and potential users.

FUTURE INQUIRY

We turn now to a discussion of future research. Although we believe that ours is an important investigation, far more information is needed about the various forms of educational computing and their determinants. In order to gather solid information, we will need a variety of both qualitative and quantitative designs, some to explore educational computing in natural settings, others to examine educational computing under controlled conditions, and both to inform each other. By analogy, the lines of research proposed in this section could be extended to other home educational technologies.

We would start with in-depth qualitative studies that can shed light on the validity of the model presented in this book. Are the conditions depicted in this model – the role of parental encouragement and aid, the school's emphasis, and the receptivity of children and their peers and siblings – central in other groups of families throughout the country and, if not, why not?[6] Do other important conditions exist – for instance, the ages of children or family socioeconomic status?

At the same time, extensive surveys could establish whether the proportions falling into the four types of families in our research persist today throughout the country among families with home computers and what the potential is for children's educational computing. Such work could also determine whether parents were working in tandem with the schools or apart from them. This information could be used to determine whether the educational promise of the home computer is being fulfilled more so now than before.

We also need more surveys and case studies on prevailing home–school relations surrounding the computer. Has the home–school connection with regard to educational computing changed and, if so, in what ways and why? Are teachers more willing to assign homework that can be done on computers than they have been in the past? Are they using computers more today for instructional purposes and, if so, is this being communicated to parents?

One particularly heuristic kind of home–school research could be based on the current array of computer collaborations among companies, schools, and homes, mentioned elsewhere in this book, such as ACOT and the Buddy System. Although some research on home–school computer collaborations has been done, we know of none using the perspective presented in our book. What would qualitative investigations show about utilization in homes and the factors that facilitate it or continue to act as obstacles even in computer-supportive environments?

Still other areas of research are discussed below: computer equity, planned technological change, and educational computing outcomes.

COMPUTER EQUITY STUDIES

One of the most thorny issues about home computers and their educational uses relates to family socioeconomic status. Up to now, the typical family purchasing a home computer has been predominantly middle class and white. Is this situation changing? If so, what are the current trends? To what extent are less affluent families purchasing home computers for their children? Does family socioeconomic status or ethnicity make a *major* difference in the home dynamics connected with educational computing, and, if so, in what ways?[7]

Strong gender differences have been noted since the beginning of the personal computer movement. Are these differences changing? Are women's attitudes about home computing changing in comparison with those of men? If so, in what ways? If they are not, then what are the dynamics behind the stability? Are younger women and school-aged girls avoiding the computer as much as the previous generation of mothers? If not, what forces have precipitated the change?

Learning disabilities are the basis of still another kind of inequality. Comparative studies of learning disabled and non-disabled children who use the computer might produce valuable insights. Are children with learning disabilities and their parents more likely to be receptive to the uses of computers for learning, especially at home, than those in the normal range? If so, what kinds of uses do they favor? What is it about computer learning that fosters their greater interest and use?

PLANNED CHANGE STUDIES

Other comparative studies of families of the learning disabled and families in the normal range can shed considerable light on the processes of diffusion, adoption, and implementation of educational computing. Are these three processes different for the population of families of the learning disabled? Does diffusion spread more widely? Does adoption come at a faster pace? Is implementation more serious and lasting? Are planned change desiderata more prevalent within the disabled target population? If the answers are in the affirmative, then what obstacles present in mainstream homes are missing? What facilitators are present with greater frequency? Put another way, are the dynamics of diffusion, adoption, and implementation different between the two types of families, and, if so, how?

In-depth qualitative work could be devoted to the study of schools as linking agents and teachers as local facilitators. Are some schools and teachers more effective than others? What conditions determine their effectiveness? As linking agents or local facilitators, what do they do with families? Is the general nature of home–school communications an important factor in understanding what makes some schools and teachers more effective than others?

Both qualitative and quantitative investigations could focus on the activities of linking agents other than schools. Are other linking agents emerging to bridge the gaps in the diffusion, adoption, and utilization of software for academic tutoring and as academic tools? If so, what are they, and how extensive are they? How successful are they in fostering home educational computing when compared to schools and why?

Still other diffusion and utilization work might be devoted to software studies. We need more accurate estimates of the amounts of educational software being purchased and the kinds of families making the purchases. We need solid information about the rates of purchase of specific pieces and the kinds of educational software. Comparative analyses of the diffusion, adoption, and implementation of different pieces of software hold great promise for understanding the processes that make some programs hits while so many remain misses.

Because educational home computing has had a long enough history, social change studies can now establish the extent to which academic computing has become institutionalized in families. At the time of our study, implementation was as far as we could go because of the newness of educational computing. Now we can ask whether younger siblings follow in the footsteps of older brothers and sisters in Type IV families. Is this way of learning passed on from sibling to sibling? What are the dynamics behind the transfer or nontransfer? What steps are parents taking to *sustain* the home use of computers for education?

STUDIES OF OUTCOMES

We need more experimental evidence about whether specific educational software programs work with children and, if so, *how* they work – the actual step-by-step process – at home in the presence of parents. Such work would have to pay close attention to the quality of a program's implementation – the enacted social envelope – as well as to its learning and motivational outcomes. What do parents and children do to foster or inhibit a program's effects? Another effort could focus on establishing what kinds of theory-driven, educational programs there are and whether software based on one kind of theory is more effective than software based on other theories. How these programs would reshape various layers of the home's social envelope would be a central question for such work.

We also need to know more about current "Nintendo" uses. Have these replaced the heavy use of personal computers for the playing of games? If so, are more personal computers gathering dust or occupying closet space? Some work might also be devoted to assessing whether families are developing an interest in new educational technologies such as multimedia and telecommunications and whether such interest dampens family involvement with simple home educational computing. Finally, we might begin to do some cross-cultural analyses. What is home educational computing like in other countries? In what ways is it similar to or different from that in the United States and why?

Although we have just served up a full platter of research possibilities, many others remain unmentioned. Nevertheless, with sound research methods, the pursuit of any one of these possibilities will yield valuable information on the development of this fascinating educational technology – the home computer.

The prominent sociologist William Fielding Ogburn was a pioneer in the study of technologies and the social trends they led to in society.[8] An astute observer of the American scene during the early and middle decades of the twentieth century, he adopted the phrase "cultural lag" to capture what happens when a technology is introduced. Our book isolates one educational instance of cultural lag, namely, the discrepancy between the personal computer as a promising breakthrough technology and the ensuing social reality still void of much academic or other educational use at home or at school. We hope our work has contributed to an understanding of what happened to cause cultural lag in this instance and what directions might be taken to help reduce it in the case of home educational computing and in the case of other promising technologies in the future.

NOTES

1. There is another whole genre of promising educational technology for the home that is also computer-based but that uses modems for educational telecommunications. We have included examples of educational home telecommunicating at different points in the book. But we do not examine this kind of educational technology in depth. The choice of "interactive multimedia" as our example rather than "telecommunications" should not be seen as an indication that we believe one is more promising as a home educational technology than the other.
2. Others include "In the Holy Land," one on AIDS, and one on Dr. Martin Luther King (see "In the Holy Land," 1989; Marriott, 1991; Lehrer, 1989).

3. Two teachers in California created their own videodisc, "Grapevine," with accompanying HyperCard stack, as background material for "The Grapes of Wrath": "There are essays, photographs, film footage, documentaries, and background information"; these include "letters from Steinbeck, Dorothea Lange's depression photographs, newsreels of dust bowl devastation and political conventions, excerpts from radio soap operas and comedy programs, the voice of F.D.R. giving his first Fireside Chat, a North Dakota farm girl's oral history of her memories of the dust bowl, maps, charts, newspaper clippings, and more" (Solomon, 1989, pp. 18–19). Hanlon, one of the teachers, says, "'Grapevine is designed to transport the user to a critical and interesting period in history and to reveal the many facets of it for further exploration'" (Solomon, 1989, p. 18). Students create their own projects using these materials.

The Texas State Board of Education in the fall of 1990 approved as a textbook Optical Data Corporation's videodisc-based elementary science curriculum, entitled "Windows on Science." "The decision marks the first time that a videodisc program . . . has been allowed to compete head-to-head with standard textbooks in a state curriculum" (Allen, 1990). Some educators believe that other states may begin to accept such programs.

4. MS-DOS computer manufacturers are currently making an effort to agree on specifications for a multimedia personal computer. Recently, twelve hardware and software companies formed the Multimedia PC Marketing Council and, at a presentation in the fall of 1991, demonstrated over sixty multimedia products. They have decided that the necessary hardware for an MPC (Multimedia Personal Computer) would be "a CD-ROM drive, audio board, Microsoft Windows with multi-media extensions, and audio output" ("Multimedia Takes Personal Computing by Storm," 1992, p. 8).

5. In the remainder of this chapter we use "multimedia" to refer to "interactive multimedia."

6. We propose this kind of work even though we know full well that first-rate, qualitative field studies of families are extremely hard to do. The main reasons are that family life is highly private and researchers have difficulty not only gaining entrance into it but also maintaining rapport and access over long stretches of time without appearing to be intruders. In addition, the work is intensive and they must be able to go into the field for extended periods.

7. Current knowledge about children's educational computing at home and the role of parents is based primarily on the study of middle-class and upper-middle-class families. Obviously, the study of less affluent families, as they acquire home computers, will enlarge our general picture of children's educational computing at home. Some might argue that less affluent parents will be more likely to *press* their children into doing educational computing, especially around the drill and practice of basic academic skills and knowledge. One reason is related to the curricula of the schools their children often attend, which seem to be more likely to stress computers for the drill and practice of basic math and reading skills. Knowing that their children's schools emphasize computers for such purposes, parents might try to do the same at home. Another reason has to do with parents' independent perceptions of their children's academic needs. Less affluent parents might worry more that their children are "behind," and, hence, in need of home academic computing, independent of school. And even further, if parents have poor math and reading skills, they might see the advantage of using the computer for their *own* academic learning as well as the value of helping their children use their home computers for learning the three R's.

   On the other hand, if more affluent parents, especially mothers, are wary of computers, it seems unlikely that less affluent parents will react much differently. Moreover, the level of their educational skills may make many feel less able or confident than their middle-class counterparts do to act as effective computer role models, coaches, or scaffolders. In addition, factors such as software expense, English reading difficulties, and the lack of time at home in the evenings with children may loom even larger in less affluent families. Finally, we doubt that children from less affluent families are any more receptive to the learning of academic subjects on their computers at home in the afternoons and evenings and on the weekends than are their middle-class counterparts.

   With these issues in mind, the comparison of more affluent and less affluent families is an area that provides a rich opportunity for studying aspects of educational computing as well as the effects of social status on family behavior.

8. See Del Sesto (1983) for an incisive review of Ogburn's theorizing about and research on technology and social change.

Appendix A

A Further Note on SITE Fieldwork and Analysis

FIELDWORKERS AND THEIR FIELDWORK EFFORTS

All of the fieldworkers were doctoral students from the various programs in the School of Education at New York University, and all were enrolled in course work in preparation for engaging in qualitative research. All were accomplished women and men with established careers in such areas as educational technology, teaching, school administration, nursing, and various allied specialties throughout the school. During their fieldwork, these doctoral students were supervised by the senior author or by other faculty or qualified staff associated with the SITE project.

The fieldworkers selected and studied families with whom they had no previous social ties. A selected family had to have at least one school-aged child living at home and had to have a computer at home. Fieldworkers informed families that the nature of their computer use was *not* an important criterion for their inclusion in the study. This strategy of selection, it was hoped, would allow us to study widely varying families, especially with regard to the educational computing of their children. Subsequent experience showed that, in fact, it did.

Each fieldworker used social contacts, school connections, and even such impersonal tactics as going to local computer stores in order to locate and select families. Since fieldworkers lived in the tristate area surrounding New York University and since they needed to make regular home visits, the final decision about which family to select was influenced by accessibility as well as the aforementioned criteria. Most fieldworkers were able to gain entrance into and establish rapport with their first-choice family. This usually took anywhere from two to three weeks. However, some did have false starts and had to make a second, and in a few cases a third, effort to contact and secure an appropriate family. Nearly all selected families were strangers to the fieldworkers. In the few instances in which the family was known to the fieldworker, special care was taken during the various phases of the research to ensure that their familiarity did not bias what was observed and reported. No one was permitted to study relatives or close friends.

All families were guaranteed anonymity. This meant that all identities were masked in all log materials and in discussions with SITE personnel. Fieldworkers also made it clear to their chosen families that they had the option of discontinuing participation at any time during the study. None of the seventy families withdrew. While several families seemed eager to end the period of fieldwork visits as quickly as possible, most families looked forward to and enjoyed their times with the fieldworkers.

A dozen or so fieldworkers also observed children in their schools and in other settings to document their out-of-home computer activities. In addition, the first eighteen families were interviewed again in the fall of 1985, roughly one year after the initial study, to ascertain whether any major changes had occurred in their computing activities. By and large, these follow-up interviews with families did not uncover any major changes, although there were a few minor changes in computing efforts. These minor changes usually amounted to less intensive computer efforts or the purchase of some new equipment, most frequently printers. A list of individual technical reports based on these first cases is presented at the end of the appendix.

The fieldworkers met on a weekly basis in support groups. These groups, composed of four to six fieldworkers, helped sustain members when field activities became stressful and helped give direction to subsequent observations and interviews. Frequently, group members also provided each other with corroborative or alternative interpretations of observations and interviews. These group reactions stimulated thinking and often provided fieldworkers with different perspectives on what they were seeing and hearing in the field.

All log entries were read by a supervising professor or staff member. Reactions to the content as well as the form of log entries were shared with fieldworkers. Suggestions regarding future tactics were also made in written feedback to the fieldworkers.

MORE ON THE CONTENT ANALYSIS OF THE LOG MATERIALS

Some of the sections of the seventeen-page codebook required a simple check or notation of the number of occurrences, while other sections required that key excerpts from the logs be included as evidence. There were codes for assessing the relative strength, from high to low, on each factor thought to affect the frequency of home academic computing as well as codes for assessing the actual degree of academic computing efforts of children. Other areas of analysis included family context, hardware and software, forms of computing, major and minor users, and the effects of usage.

After the first of the seventy cases was analyzed, the remaining case logs were divided among the team members. The senior author and a research associate reviewed each case analysis as it was completed, either concurring with or raising issues about various coding judgments. The analysts would then respond to the queries in an attempt to arrive at a consensus. If no clear agreement could be reached, the issue would be discussed at the next team meeting. At these meetings, the team would decide how to code the troublesome or conflicting findings. This coding process took a substantial amount of time, and always involved three sources or anchor points: the original fieldworker's analysis of his or her log, the team member's independent log evaluation, and the review by some member or members of the coding team. After ratings for all the families were completed, families were grouped into four categories by level of their children's home educational computing. These four groups were then compared to determine the relative presence of the various explanatory conditions.

UNPUBLISHED TECHNICAL REPORTS
COMPLETED BY FIELDWORKERS AFTER
THE FIRST YEAR OF THE SITE STUDY, 1985

Benesch, S. Exercising restraint: The Lawrence family (49 pp.).
Blaustein, E. Losing the appetite to byte: The Brien family (36 pp.).
Carroll, R. Great anticipations: The Thomas family (38 pp.).
Danish, B. Following the leader and beyond: The Knelli-Schwartz family (63 pp.).
Friedman, H. Microcomputers on a grand scale: The Holland family (30 pp.).
Lane, P. A. You can lead a horse to water, but . . . : The Redd family (30 pp.).
Lefton, M. Ripples not waves: The Nadel family (40 pp.).
Lizzul, R. An educational enterprise: The Frascati family (46 pp.).
Moinester, D. Great expectations – modest realizations: The Gaines family (46 pp.).
Oliver, N. To empower, to emulate, but not to educate: The O'Day family (36 pp.).
Sanger, L. A matter of culture: The Min family (34 pp.).
Schall, P. Challenges: The Carson family (59 pp.).
Scher, S. A major league dream: The Ernest family (44 pp.).
Schine, R. Humanism and the computer, strange bedfellows: The Darrow family (36 pp.).
Smaller, A. "The right stuff": The Jameson family (30 pp.).
Sokoll, D. Investing in the future: The Adams family (27 pp.).

List of Codes for Site Log Analysis

Family Context **[FAMCON]**
  a. physical surroundings such as
      home, neighborhood, town or city,
      general geographic area   FAMCON.PHY
  b. social background and individual
      features of family members   FAMCON.SOC
  c. internal social relations:
      parent–parent, child–parent;
      child–child   FAMCON.INT
  d. external social relations:
      work, friends, relatives   FAMCON.EXT

Home Microcomputing Resources **[HO]**
  a. home hardware   HOHW.
        the machine   .MC
        ancillary hardware   .ANC
        location   .LOC
  b. home software   HOSW.
        games   .GM
        academics   .AC
        programming   .PR
        wordprocessing   .WP
        other   .OT
  c. home magazines   HOMAG.
        subscriptions   .SUB
        occasional purchase or
           use of other sources   .OCA
        missing   .MIS

Microcomputer Adoption **[AD]**
  a. main purpose behind adoption   ADPUR.
        primarily for children's
           education   .ED
        predominantly work-related   .WK

	a mix of work and	
	children's education	.MX
	other	.OT
b.	major person behind adoption	ADPER.
	father	.FA
	mother	.MO
	child	.CH
	mix of parents and children	.MX
	someone outside the family	.OS

Microcomputing Efforts **[EFF]**

a.	child's effort	CHEFF.
	gaming	.GM
	academic study	.ACM
	word processing	.WD
	programming	.PR
	missing	.MIS
b.	parental effort	PAREFF.
	work-related	.WK
	recreational	.REC
	home-related	.HO
	other	.OT
	missing	.MIS

Factors behind Extent of Children's Academic Microcomputing Efforts

a.	parental antecedents, in general	PARAN.GEN
b.	parental antecedents, microcomputer-related	PARAN.MC
c.	parental antededents, ACM-related	PARAN.ACM
d.	parental pressure and support for ACM	PARPS.ACM
e.	school pressure and support for ACM	SCHPS.ACM
f.	peer pressure and support for ACM	PERPS.ACM
g.	sibling pressure and support for ACM	SIBPS.ACM
h.	home software that is academic in nature	HOSW. ACM
i.	child experience with ACM	CHEX.ACM
j.	child receptivity to ACM	CHREC.ACM

Consequences of Home Microcomputing **[MICCONS]**

a.	on children	.CH
b.	on parents	.PAR

    c. on interpersonal family relations   .FAM

    d. in other ways   .OT

    e. discernible consequences missing   .MIS

"Third Position" codes that apply to all existing codes

    a. conflicting evidence   .CONF

    b. inaccurate statements by subjects   .INA

    c. other   .OT

Other Related Codes

    a. a new factor behind ACM   NEWFAC.ACM

    b. extent of home/school hardware
       compatibility   HOSCH.HW

    c. peer pressure re: extent of HW
       compatibility   PERPS.HW

    d. peer pressure for computing
       other than ACM   PERPS.MC

    e. mastery of the computer's OS   EFF.OS

    f. research project's effect
       on CHs or PAs   REEFF.CH; PAR

    g. competence of CH or PA
       with the computer   COMP.CH; PAR

Appendix C

Site Log Analysis Codebook

Reviewer Initials_____
Date(s):_____
Log #_____
I. *Family Context* [FAMCON]
[FAMCON.BAC]
Surname Pseudonym_____

	Pseudonym	Occupation	Age		Living at Home
Father	_____	_____	_____		_____
Mother	_____	_____	_____		_____
Other Adult	_____	_____	_____		_____

	Pseudonym	Gender	Age	Grade	School Type [Public/Private]
					_____
Children at Home	_____	_____	_____	_____	_____
	_____	_____	_____	_____	_____
	_____	_____	_____	_____	_____
	_____	_____	_____	_____	_____
Children not Home	_____	_____	_____	_____	_____
	_____	_____	_____	_____	_____
	_____	_____	_____	_____	_____
	_____	_____	_____	_____	_____

[FAMCON.PHY,SOC,INT,EXT]
Location of Home: City, Suburb, Rural.
Family SES: Professional/Upper-middle Class; Middle; Blue Collar; Lower.
Other key points regarding this family, its social/physical setting, its internal and/or external social relations, or its individual members' features.

Appendix C

II. *Adoption of Microcomputer* [AD]
        Major Purpose(s) [ADPUR]
        Key People Involved in Adoption [ADPER]

III. *Home Hardware* [HOHW]
[HOHW.MIC]

Microcomputer Brand and Model	Date Purchased
_____	_____
_____	_____
_____	_____
	_____

[HOHW.ANC]
Peripherals (Put the Number of
  Each on the Line):

TV Set	_____
Monochrome Monitors	_____
Color Monitors	_____
Disc Drives	_____
Cassette Drives	_____
Printers	_____
Koala Pads	_____
Joysticks	_____
Modems	_____
Other(s)	_____
	_____

Location of Microcomputer(s) at Home:

IV. *Home Software* [HOSW]

Software	# of Packages	Names of Most Often Used
Games [HOSW.GM]	_____	_____
Programming [HOSW.PR]	_____	_____
Academic [HOSW.AC]**	_____	_____
Word processing [HOSW.WP]	_____	_____
Other [HOSW.OT]		
_____	_____	_____
_____	_____	_____
_____	_____	_____

** Include game formatted packages – edutainment.
Key family thoughts about software, especially the meaning of ACSW (or
  other educational) software: Give direct statements and their citations.
Home Computer Magazine Subscriptions [HOMAG]

V. *Microcomputing Efforts by Children and/or Parents* [CHEFF, PAREFF]
Home Microcomputing:

Pseudonym(s)

Major User(s) _____
Minor User(s) _____
Non-User(s)   _____

	Ch	Ch	Ch	Ch			Fa	Mo
Games	___	___	___	___	Work		___	___
Prgrmng	___	___	___	___	Recreation		___	___
Wrdprcssng	___	___	___	___	Home		___	___
Acdmcs	___	___	___	___	Family		___	___
Other	___	___	___	___	Other		___	___

KEY: Leave blank, if none
      L = little (sporadic)
      S = some (once a week on average)
      M= much (2 to 3 times a week on average)
      ??= insufficient evidence

Categorize the family according to this schema (check one):
_____ A family where academic software and child microcomputing were absent
_____ A family without academic software where child microcomputing occurred, though not for academic study
_____ A family with academic software where child microcomputing did not involve academic study
_____ A family where academic microcomputing was tried and abandoned
_____ A family where academic microcomputing occurred sporadically
_____ A family where light, regular academic microcomputing occurred
_____ A family where heavy, regular academic microcomputing occurred

Key quotes and/or observations that reflect the level of child efforts to do academic microcomputing: [CHEFF.ACM]

VI. *Facilitators and/or Obstacles to CHEFF.ACM at Home*
(Circle each appropriate rating: H=High; M=Moderate; L=Low)
  1. General Parental Antecedents [PARAN.GEN]
     Overall Parental Rating: +H M L Missing L M H–
          Mother   +H M L Missing L M H–
          Give examples and citations
          Father   +H M L Missing L M H–
          Give examples and citations

  2. Microcomputing-related Parental Antecedents [PARAN.MC]
     Overall Parental Rating: +H M L Missing L M H–

Mother   +H M L Missing L M H–
Give examples and citations
Father   +H M L Missing L M H–
Give examples and citations

3. Academic Microcomputing-specific Parental Antecendents [PARAN.ACM]
Overall Parental Rating: +H M L Missing L M H–
    Mother   +H M L Missing L M H–
    Give examples and citations
    Father   +H M L Missing L M H–
    Give examples and citations

4. Parental Pressure and Support for ACM [PARPS.ACM]
Overall Parental Rating: +H M L Missing L M H–
    Mother   +H M L Missing L M H–
    Give examples and citations
    Father   +H M L Missing L M H–
    Give examples and citations

5. Children's School Emphasis on ACM [SCHPS.ACM]
    Rating   +H M L Missing L M H–
    Give examples and citations
6. Children's Peer Pressure to Engage in ACM [PERPS.ACM]
    Rating   +H M L Missing L M H–
    Give examples and citations

7. Sibling Support for ACM [SIBPS.ACM]
    Rating   +H M L Missing L M H–
    Give examples and citations
8. Academic Software at Home [HOSW.ACM]
    Rating   +H M L Missing L M H–
    Give examples and citations

9. Children's Prior Experience with ACM and the Basic Quality of that Experience [CHEX.ACM]
    Rating   +H M L Missing L M H–
    Give examples and citations
10. Children's Receptivity to Academic Learning on the Micro at Home [CHREC.ACM.HO]
    Rating   +H M L Missing L M H–
    Give examples and citations

VII. *Does this Case Confirm the Proposed ACM Model?*
Yes, Fully   Yes, Partially   Uncertain   No
Explain below:

VIII. *Were there Other Central Factors or Conditions in this Family that Affected CHEFF.ACM?*
Yes   Uncertain   No
IF YES: elaborate below:

IX. *In Your Own Words, Why Did or Why Did Not ACM Take Hold in this Family?*
Elaborate below:

X. *Microcomputing Consequences* [MICCON]
In your own words, how would you characterize the influence of microcomputers on family members, on the family as a unit, on the family in general, and on the children educationally?

XI. *Irrespective of ACM, were there other meaningful ways that the microcomputer(s) was (were) being used in this family setting?*
Yes   No
IF YES, elaborate:
IF NO, how would you characterize use?
_____ Parents were distanced from the microcomputer and children only used it for recreational purposes
_____ The microcomputer was rarely used by anyone for any purpose
_____ Other (specify)

XII. *Were there Any Blockbuster Quotes?*
Yes   No
IF YES, present them below verbatim and with log citations:

XIII. *List below the Major Hypotheses or Questions that Emerged from Your Analysis:*

Authors' Note: The actual seventeen-page codebook had many large open spaces throughout for the writing of comments. These have been removed in this version.

Appendix D

List of Families and School-Aged Children

	Father, Age and Occupation		Mother, Age and Occupation		Daughters, Ages	Sons, Ages	Resi-dence	Eth-nicity
01	30s	Bank Officer	30s	PS Teacher	–	14,11	NYC	W
02	30s	Computer Spc	30s	Homemaker	11	9	NYC	W
03	30s	US Gov Offcr	30s	Homemaker	–	15,11	CT	W
04	50s	Business Offcr	50s	Homemaker	–	13	CT	W
05	30s	Systems Anlyst	30s	PS Teacher	15	18	NYS	W
06	30s	Salesman	30s	Homemaker	–	11,8,7	NYS	W
07	–	Not Present	40s	Psychologist	–	14	NYS	W
08	30s	HS Principal	30s	PS Teacher	16,13	–	NYS	W
09	40s	CPA	40s	Homemaker	–	17	CT	W
10	50s	Sm Bs Owner	30s	Book Editor	12	9	NYS	W
11	30s	Lawyer	30s	Bib Editor	8,5	–	NYC	W
12	30s	Computer Spc	30s	Homemaker	7	5	NYC	A
13	–	Not Present	40s	Art Bs Owner	5	14,11,10	NYS	W
14	30s	Professor	30s	Homemaker	11	–	NYS	W
15	30s	Sm Bs Owner	30s	Sm Bs Owner	9,6	–	NYS	H
16	40s	Physician	30s	Homemaker	12	11	CT	W
17	50s	Business VP	40s	Homemaker	–	14,10	NJ	W
18	40s	Business Offcr	40s	Homemaker	16	13	NYC	W
19	40s	Professor	–	Not Present	–	16	NYC	W
20	40s	Computer Exec	40s	Prgmer	–	11,7	NYC	W
21	50s	Corp Trainer	40s	Real Est Sales	–	15	NJ	W
22	50s	Nwspr Editor	40s	Social Wrkr	12	15	NYC	W
23	40s	Court Lawyer	30s	Occup Thrpst	–	15,12	NYS	W
24	40s	Market Conslt	40s	Libr Asstnt	10	17	CT	W
25	40s	Professor	40s	Social Wrkr	12	15	NYC	W
26	30s	RR Conslt	30s	Social Wrkr	9	6	NYC	W
27	50s	Elvtr Operatr	50s	Seamstress	17	–	NYC	H
28	40s	PS Dept Chr	40s	Programmer	11	–	NYC	W
29	30s	Professor	30s	Homemaker	–	9	NJ	W
30	30s	PS Teacher	30s	Homemaker	15	13	NYS	W
31	50s	Check Casher	50s	Retail Clerk	–	16	NYC	W
32	30s	Lab Techncn	30s	PS Teacher	5	–	NYC	B

Appendix D

	Father, Age and Occupation		Mother, Age and Occupation		Daughters, Ages	Sons, Ages	Resi- dence	Eth- nicity
33	50s	Magz Editor	40s	SocSer Conslt	17	–	NYC	W
34	40s	Professor	30s	Lawyer	–	16	NYC	W
35	50s	Ad Agncy Dir	40s	Play Thrpst	9	13	NYC	W
36	40s	Comptroller	40s	PS Teacher	16,7	–	NYC	W
37	40s	Elec Techncn	30s	Chef	8	11	NYC	B
38	40s	Programmer	30s	Homemaker	15,13,10	5	NYC	W
39	40s	Professor	40s	PS Teacher	–	12	NYC	W
40	40s	Clergyman	40s	Homemaker	–	13	NYS	W
41	40s	Professor	30s	Homemaker	9	6	NYS	W
42	40s	Retail Mngr	40s	PS Teacher	6	–	NYS	W
43	40s	Photog Conslt	40s	SocWk Supvsr	–	12	NYC	W
44	30s	Printer	30s	Social Wrkr	12	10	NYC	W
45	30s	PS Teacher	30s	PS Teacher	5	–	NYS	W
46	40s	Computer Exec	40s	Film Editor	–	8	NYC	W
47	50s	Phone Co Techn	50s	Waitress	16	13	NYC	W
48	40s	Accountant	40s	PS Teacher	15,15	*	NJ	W
49	40s	Mngmnt Conslt	30s	Homemaker	5	–	NYC	W
50	30s	Energy Conslt	30s	Homemaker	10,8,7	–	NJ	W
51	40s	Banker	40s	Homemaker	6	13,10	NYS	W
52	30s	Cmptr Prgmr	30s	Lawyer	–	6	NJ	W
53	40s	Professor	40s	Sales	10	14	NYC	W
54	40s	Cmptr Bs Owner	40s	Business Exec	–	13	NYC	W
55	40s	PS Teacher	30s	PS Teacher	10,9	–	NJ	W
56	50s	TV Prodcr/Dir	40s	Actress	17,15	–	NYC	W
57	40s	Intr Decorator	40s	PS Teacher	–	13	NYC	W
58	40s	Bsnss Owner	40s	Homemaker	–	7	NYC	W
59	40s	Professor	40s	PS Teacher	–	11,8	NYC	W
60	–	Not Present	40s	Bsnss Owner	–	13,11	NJ	A
61	40s	Systms Managr	40s	Homemaker	14	17	NYC	W
62	40s	Programmer	40s	Homemaker	–	12,11,9	NYS	W
63	40s	Dentist	40s	Homemaker	–	16,11	NYC	W
64	40s	Bank Conslt	40s	Exec Secrtry	13,7	15	NYC	B
65	–	Not Present	30s	Bank Secrtry	–	16,10	NYC	B
66	30s	Salesman	30s	Homemaker	–	5	NYS	W
67	40s	Cmptr Exec	30s	Bank Teller	12	15	NYS	W
68	30s	DataPrc Managr	30s	Nurse	11,9	–	NJ	W
69	50s	Professor	40s	Bookkeeper	–	17	NYC	W
70	–	Not Present	40s	Artist	13	–	NYS	W

Note: NYC = The five boroughs: Bronx, Brooklyn, Manhattan, Queens, and Staten Island. NYS = Surrounding areas of New York State: Long Island, Rockland County, and Westchester County. Ethnicity: A = Asian, B = Black, H = Hispanic, W = White.
* This family had five school-aged boys: 18, 17, 12, 10, 5.

Appendix E

Specific Steps Families Might Take

As we indicated in Chapter 12, during the course of writing this book, we had a variety of thoughts about concrete steps that might help parents and children use their home computers for education. In this appendix, we present some of these ideas along with some readings that might be of assistance to them.

CREATORS AND PRODUCERS

The creators and producers of academic software could redouble their efforts to conceptualize role behaviors of parents that would facilitate children's use of their educational software at home. They could build these thoughts into "guidelines for the home" to accompany software. The design of the software itself could incorporate a structure that at least encourages parental involvement and support. Software companies could also provide effective in-service training of software salespersons, who in turn could better assist parents in the choice and use of academic software.

Producers might make children's educational software more appealing to adults as well. An excellent and familiar example is Children's Television Workshop's "Sesame Street," which incorporates humor and information that parents appreciate. In this way, parents might be encouraged to watch and help children use educational software at home.

Producers and designers, with the help of educational researchers, could design products that would enable parents to structure learning experiences for their children. There are examples of teams of applied researchers and producers working together to produce multimedia learning environments. With the aid of such a team, product development can be shaped by the actual use of the technology in real social contexts.

In addition, producers could become more mindful of issues of hardware design. Portability, compatibility of equipment, obsolescence, start-up time to learn a new system – all of these issues are of concern to parents and need to be more successfully addressed in the marketplace.

LINKING AGENTS

Whether it is the school or some other linking agent or some combination of local facilitators, including the school, families need help in a variety of ways. For example, linking agents could help parents assess their needs and assist in their purchase of software and hardware by creating software and hardware libraries, by arranging educational discounts for group purchases, and by mapping out possible locations in the home for computing.

Linking agents might also arrange to lend appropriate software to families and to organize ways in which families could sell software their children have outgrown. Schools, libraries, and museums, for example, might consider establishing software lending libraries for families; informal learning institutions can develop workshops or training programs in technological use for teams of children and parents; projects begun at community fairs can be designed for completion at home, with clear guidance to parents; assistance hotlines, newsletters, and computer bulletin boards can be made available; and organizations can help foster parent clubs, user groups, or teams of parent advisors that would aid in keeping parents knowledgeable about critical issues in technological use.

Local facilitators can institute workshops for parents. These workshops might have a positive influence on parental (especially mothers') reactions to computers by clarifying for parents what educational computing means and by helping them develop the skills needed in order to help their children gain from educational computer use. In this way, the facilitator might build on the positive conception parents already seem to have about the importance of computers in the future, helping them to see that their children could gain from the use of computers in the present.

Workshops could also encourage parents to pay attention to the patterns of social interaction around the computer and could show them how parental roles can change. They could make parents aware that they can provide help through goal setting, modeling, coaching, scaffolding, and praising. They could inform parents about the current interest in collaborative and open-ended learning and could help them understand how computers facilitate such learning. They could also make parents aware of gender patterns and issues of equity.

Since there are many educational uses for computers and since families often differ in their needs, there are many possible patterns to follow. Families need to be informed about how home use might correspond with school. Parents, in turn, could play an active role in this process. They need to let the school know that they are interested and they would like to give input. At the same time, they would need to let the school know that they would welcome help in learning all about the educational uses of computers at home.

Schools, especially, might show parents who are familiar with computers to some extent how they can use their software with their children. For example, parents and children might be encouraged to use a word processor to write newsletters about family events, a spreadsheet to keep track of baseball statistics or how an allowance is spent, and a data base to make an address book or to catalogue a child's book or record collection. With other families, it may be enough at the beginning to help parents understand that their children can benefit from using computers and to lead them to oversee, support, and acknowledge their children's educational computer use. Parents who are reluctant to use computers may be encouraged to play games with their children and to have their children teach them something about the computer. Perhaps some parents can be taught how to take advantage of what games have to offer and can learn how to discuss these games with their children, helping them to recognize the strategies they use and to transfer some of their learning to other domains.

FAMILIES HELPING THEMSELVES

Although the average family needs a lot of help, those who have an interest in home educational computing can help themselves in a number of ways. They can start by examining their own values and priorities as these are related to the allocation of time, effort, and money. Serious educational computing at home might mean a substantial reallocation of resources. If, indeed, a family decides to make children's educational computing at home a priority and expects to integrate this technology into their vision of family education and empowerment, then new attitudes and new behaviors will be required.

There are many ways in which parents can try to acquire the knowledge and orientation needed for using the computer at home educationally with their children. But first, parents will need to be receptive to training – training to familiarize themselves with available and required hardware and software related to education. Parents may need to seek new knowledge about learning and motivation theories and about developmental readiness – especially as they relate to gender – in order to identify and create informal learning situations for their children. They might benefit from forming or joining – if they exist – educational user groups.

Also, families may need to make conscious decisions about ergonomic issues such as the home location and management of the computer and its software. It might be useful for them to consider such questions as: Where will equipment be placed? Who will be responsible for maintenance? How will software be purchased and updated?

Parents might do well to remind themselves to start with realistic short-term goals, and to build progressively as their knowledge and skills evolve. By accepting their own starting points and then being willing to experiment, they might be able to foster more mindful attitudes toward the use of computers for education.

If they are going to help their children they may have to consider developing more collaborative relationships with them, at least around the computer – especially given the fact that children on the whole tend to know more about computers than many parents. Some specific and easy first steps for parents and children might be to (1) become familiar with word processing by using it for joint correspondence to family and friends; (2) ask their children to teach them computer games; or (3) purchase software that a child is familiar with through school and allow the child to teach it to them and to siblings.

Families might consider how the home can be used for computer-related teaching instead of just expecting the transfer of school practices into homes. In this way, families could think about ways to use the computer that would enhance what they already do as a group such as scheduling, planning a budget, and record-keeping. They could use the home computer for hobbies and family projects such as planning a trip, doing a family tree, or writing a family history. Also, family members could spend time just sitting and watching what other members do at the computer, thereby extending the time together as a family unit. By placing computer learning and use into an everyday context of intrinsically meaningful activities, both parents and children are likely to receive immediate reinforcement for their computing efforts.

Perhaps more daunting than buying a computer and the ancillary hardware is the task of evaluating the usefulness and appropriateness of particular software for their children. This is not an easy task since there are literally thousands of hard-to-find and hard-to-sample programs and little information to help parents make wise purchases. We therefore end this addendum with a list of typical software-evaluation questions parents might use to help them decide whether a piece of software is what their child needs at this particular time in his or her educational endeavors. We include at the end, several useful references to help parents in their purchase of educational software.

SOFTWARE QUESTIONS

1. What is the title of the program?
2. What is the main topic or subject?
3. When was it created?
4. Who is the publisher?
5. What is the cost?
6. What is the age level of the intended users?
7. Does the program include a clear description of goals or objectives?
8. What is the presentation mode: game, drill and practice, tutorial, simulation, critical thinking?
9. What hardware and peripheral devices are needed or desirable in running the program?
10. What must I already know about computers in order to use the program?
11. What is the typical session time?
12. What must I do in preparation for using the program with my child?
13. Are the operating instructions easy to follow?
14. Is the accompanying documentation thorough and easy to read?
15. Is the reading level appropriate for my child's use?
16. Is the program free of grammar, spelling, and syntax errors?
17. Is the program free of stereotypes (e.g., racial, sex, ethnic)?
18. Does the pacing engage my child's attention?
19. Can we modify the program's pacing?
20. Does the program stimulate our thinking?
21. Does the program integrate my child's prior learning?
22. Will the program be easy to use under normal circumstances?
23. Are "help" screens available?
24. Can the program be exited whenever desired?
25. Is record keeping built into the program?
26. Are screen displays clear and logical?
27. Are features such as color, sound, graphics, and animation included?
28. Is the format consistent from one section to another?
29. Are the feedback and rewards appropriate and helpful?

30. Does the program have interactive capabilities?
31. Are there useful branching options that allow use in a nonlinear fashion?
32. Does the program accommodate individual learning styles, age levels, or group sizes (e.g., individual use, parent–child teams)?
33. What do I like most about the program?
34. What do I like least about the program?

SOFTWARE REFERENCES

Blank, M., and Berlin, L. (1991). *The Parent's Guide to Educational Software.* Redmond, WA: Microsoft Press.

EPIE Institute. (1992). *The Latest and the Best.* Water Mill, NY.

EPIE Institute. (1985). *The Educational Software Selector.* New York: Teachers College Press.

Kids & Computers: A Magazine for Parents.

Raskin, R., and Ellison, C. *Parents, Kids & Computers.* New York: Random House Electronic Publishing.

Stewart, L., and Michael, T. (1989). *Parents Guide to Educational Software and Computers.* San Diego, CA: Computer Publishing Enterprises.

The above references – all excellent – attest to the fact that there is a growing interest in helping parents, as well as teachers, to evaluate and choose educational software. As our book was going to press, we came upon the Raskin and Ellison book and the magazine for parents. Raskin and Ellison describe many of the best educational software programs and, more important, detail concrete steps *parents* can take to encourage and assist their children. They also give suggestions for related parent–child educational activities as well as review for parents many of the issues surrounding the purchase of computer hardware. *Kids & Computers* is a new publication by Golden Empire Publications Inc., 130 Chaparral Ct., Anaheim Hills, CA 92808. It offers parents a clear philosophy about the role, value, and use of computers in the education of their children as well as practical advice about software.

References

Alcorn, P. A. (1986). *Social issues in technology.* Englewood Cliffs, NJ: Prentice-Hall.

Allen, M. (1990, November 13). Texas approves a "textbook" on videodisks. *Wall Street Journal.*

Ancarrow, J. S. (1987). *Use of computers in home study.* Washington, DC: Center for Statistics (OERI/ED).

Apple Classroom of Tomorrow. (1989). [Pamphlet]. Cupertino, CA: Advanced Technology Group, Apple Computer.

Arensberg, C. M., & Niehoff, A. H. (1964). *Introducing social change.* Chicago: Aldine.

Bacon, K. H. (1990, July 31). Many educators view involved parents as key to children's success in school. *Wall Street Journal.*

Baker, E., Gearhart, M., & Herman, J. L. (1990). *Apple classrooms of tomorrow: First- and second-year findings* (ACOT Report No. 7). Cupertino, CA: Apple Classroom of Tomorrow, Advanced Technology Group, Apple Computer, Inc.

Ballantine, J. (1989). *The sociology of education.* Englewood Cliffs, NJ: Prentice-Hall.

Bandura, A. (1977). Self-efficacy: Toward a satisfying theory of behavior change. *Psychological Review, 64,* 191–215.

Barnett, H. G. (1953). *Innovation.* New York: McGraw-Hill.

Becker, H. J. (1982, January). Microcomputers in the classroom – Dreams and realities. (Report No. 319). Baltimore, MD: Johns Hopkins University.

Becker, H. J. (1985). How schools use microcomputers: Results from a national survey. In M. Chen & W. Paisley (Eds.), *Children and microcomputers: Research on the newest medium* (pp. 87–107). Beverly Hills: Sage.

References

Becker, H. J. (1986). *Instructional uses of school computers: Reports from the 1985 national survey.* Baltimore: Johns Hopkins University.

Becker, H. J. (1987, February). Using computers for instruction. *Byte,* pp. 149–50, 152, 154, 156, 158, 160, 162.

Becker, H. J. (1991). When powerful tools meet conventional beliefs and institutional constraints. *The Computing Teacher, 18*(8), 6–9.

Berger, J. (1989, August 6). How teaching by computer played out. *New York Times,* p. 7. (Sect. 4).

Berman, E. (1985, Fall). The improbability of meaningful educational reform. *Issues in Education, 3*(2), 99–112.

Besser, H. (in press). Education as market place. In R. Muffoletto & N. Knupfer (Eds.), *Social perspectives of computers in education.* Norwood, NJ: Ablex.

Blank, M., & Berlin, L. (1991). *The parent's guide to educational software.* Redmond, WA: Microsoft.

Blau, P. M., & Scott, W. R. (1962). *Formal organizations.* San Francisco: Chandler.

Bogdan, R. C., & Biklen, S. K. (1992). *Qualitative research for education* (2nd ed.). Boston: Allyn and Bacon.

Borisoff, D., & Merrill, L. (1985). *The power to communicate: Gender differences as barriers.* Prospect Heights, IL: Waveland.

Bork, A. (1985). *Personal computers for education.* New York: Harper & Row.

Bowman, R. F. (1982). A "Pac-Man" theory of motivation: Tactical implications for classroom instruction. *Educational Technology, 22*(9), 14–16.

Brady, H. (1988, January). Piggyback programs for *Appleworks. Classroom Computer Learning,* p. 12.

Brady, H. (1989, September). Interactive multimedia: The next wave. *Classroom Computer Learning,* pp. 56–61.

Bruder, I. (1992, October). All things being equal. *Electronic Learning,* pp. 16–17.

Caldwell, R. (1986, May/June). Computer learning can begin at home. *Electronic Education,* pp. 13–15.

Calhoun, R. (1981). The microcomputer revolution? Technical possibilities and social choices. *Sociological Methods and Research, 9,* 422.

Cancian, F. (1967). Stratification and risk-taking. *American Sociological Review, 32,* 912–27.

Carlson, R. O. (1965). *Adoption of educational innovations.* Eugene, OR: Center for the Advanced Study of Educational Administration, University of Oregon.

References

Carroll, J. M. (1990). *The Nurnburg funnel: Designing minimalist instruction for practical computer skill*. Cambridge, MA: MIT Press.

Char, C. A. (1985, October 2). The potential of videodisc technology for children's learning: Research and design implications. Paper presented at the Sixth Annual Nebraska Videodisc Symposium, Lincoln, NE.

Char, C., & Wilson, K. (1986, Winter/Spring). Film making studios and Mayan ruins: Interactive video for children's learning. *Harvard Graduate School of Education Association Bulletin*, pp. 2–3.

Clement, F. J. (1981). Affective considerations in computer-based education. *Educational Technology, 21*(4), 28–32.

Coleman, J. S. (1966). *Equality of educational opportunity*. Washington, DC: U.S. Government Printing Office.

Coleman, J. S. (1987). Families and schools. *Educational Researcher, 16*(6), 32–8.

Collins, A., Brown, J. S., & Newman, S. E. (1989). Cognitive apprenticeship: Teaching the crafts of reading, writing, and mathematics. In L. B. Resnick (Ed.), *Knowing, learning, and instruction* (pp. 453–94). Hillsdale, NJ: Erlbaum.

Collis, B. (1985). Sex-related differences in attitudes toward computers: Implications for counselors. *School Counselor, 22*, 120–30.

Collis, B. (1989). Research in the application of computers in education: Trends and issues over four years of "Research Windows." Paper presented at the annual conference of the National Educational Computing Conference, Boston, MA.

Conant, J. B. (1963). *The education of American teachers*. New York: McGraw-Hill.

Cross, P. K. (1984). The rising tide of school reform reports. *Phi Delta Kappan, 66*, 167–72.

Crowson, R. L. (Ed.). (1992). *School–community relations under reform*. Berkeley: McCutchan.

Cuban, L. (1986). *Teachers and machines: The classroom use of technology since 1920*. New York: Teachers College Press.

D'Angelo, D. A., & Adler, C. R. (1991). Chapter 1: A catalyst for improving parent involvement. *Phi Delta Kappan, 72*, 350–4.

de Sola Pool, I. (1983). *Forecasting the telephone*. Norwood, NJ: Ablex.

Del Sesto, S. (1983). Technology and social change: W. F. Ogburn Revisted. *Technological Forecasting and Social Change, 24*, 183–96.

Depke, D. A. (1990, September 10). Home computers: Will they sell this time? *Business Week*, pp. 64–8, 70, 74.

References

Desai, Padma (1992, April 12). A fist full of rubles. [Review of *What is to be done?*]. *New York Times*, (Sec. 7), p. 20.

Driscoll, M. E. (1992). School–community relations and school effectiveness. In R. L. Crowson (Ed.), *School–community relations under reform* (pp. 105–27). Berkeley: McCutchan.

Dworkin, A. (1976). *Our blood: Prophesies and discourses on sexual politics*. New York: Perigee.

Educational technology 1987: A report on EL's Seventh Annual Survey of the States. (1987, October). *Electronic Learning*, pp. 39–44, 83.

Edyburn, D. L., & Lartz, M. N. (1986). The teacher's role in the use of computers in early childhood education. *Journal of the Division for Early Childhood, 10*, 255–63.

Ellison, C. (1989, January). PCs in the schools: An American tragedy. *PC Computing*, pp. 96–9, 102–4.

EPIE Institute. (1985). *T-E-S-S: The educational software selector*. New York: Teachers College Press.

EPIE Institute. (1990). *Integrated instructional systems report*. Hampton Bays, NY: The Educational Products Instructional Exchange Institute.

EPIE Institute. (1992). *The latest and the best of TESS: 1991–92 Edition*. Hampton Bays, NY: The Educational Products Instructional Exchange Institute.

Epstein, J. (1986). Parents' reactions to teacher practices of parent involvement. *The Elementary School Journal, 86*, 277–94.

Epstein, J. L. (1985). Home and school connections in schools of the future: Implications of research on parent involvement. *Peabody Journal of Education, 62*(2), 18–41.

Epstein, J. L. (1987). Toward a theory of family–school connections: Teacher practices and parent involvement. In K. Hurrelmann, F. X. Kaufmann, & F. Lösel (Eds.), *Social intervention: Potential and constraints* (pp. 121–36). New York: Gruyten.

Epstein, J. L. (1989). Family structure and student motivation: A developmental perspective. In C. Ames & R. Ames (Eds.), *Research on Motivation in Education* (pp. 259–95). Orlando: Academic.

Epstein, J. L. (1991). Paths to partnership: What we can learn from federal, state, district, and school initiatives. *Phi Delta Kappan, 72*, 344–9.

Erickson, F. (1991). Conceptions of school culture: An overview. In N. B. Wyner (Ed.), *Current perspectives on the culture of schools* (pp. 1–12). Cambridge, MA: Brookline.

References

Ferrell, K. (1987, September). Computers in the classroom: Ten years and counting. *Compute!*, pp. 12, 16, 18–20, 22–4, 28.

Ferrell, K. (1989, July). Nintendo: Just kids' play or computer in disguise? *Compute!*, pp. 28–33.

Fisher, L. M. (1988, July 19). PC makers' campaign in schools. *New York Times*, pp. D1, D11.

Fliegel, F. C., & Kivlin, J. E. (1966). Attributes of innovations as factors in diffusion. *American Journal of Sociology, 72*, 235–48.

French, L. A., Lucariello, J., Seidman, S., & Nelson, K. (1985). The influence of discourse content and context on preschoolers' use of language. In L. Galda & A. D. Pellegrini (Eds.), *Play, language, and stories: The development of children's literate behavior* (pp. 1–27). Norwood, NJ: Ablex.

From drill sergeant to intellectual assistant: Computers in the schools. (1985). *Carnegie Quarterly, 30*(3–4), 1–7.

Fullan, M. (1991). *The new meaning of educational change* (S. Stiegel-bauer, Collaborator). New York: Teachers College Press.

Garcia, D. L. (1991, Winter). Assessing the impacts of technology. *Whole Earth Review: Access to Tools and Ideas*, pp. 26–9.

Gardner, D. P. (1983). *A nation at risk*. Washington, DC: U.S. Government Printing Office.

Gerver, E., & Lewis, L. (1984). Women, computers and adult education: Liberation or oppression? *Convergence: An International Journal of Adult Education, 17*, 5–16.

Giacquinta, J. B. (1975a, Winter). Status, risk, and receptivity to innovations in complex organizations: A study of the responses of four groups of educators to the proposed introduction of sex education in elementary schools. *Sociology of Education, 48*(4), 38–58.

Giacquinta, J. B. (1975b, Fall). Status risk-taking: A central issue in the initiation and implementation of public school innovations. *Journal of Research and Development in Education, 9*(1), 102–14.

Giacquinta, J. B., & Ely, M. (1986). A longitudinal study of children's educational microcomputing at home (SITE Tech. Rep. No. 6). New York: New York University.

Giacquinta, J. B., & Lane, P. A. (1990). Fifty-one families with computers: A study of children's academic uses of microcomputers at home. *Educational Technology Research and Development, 38*(2), 27–37.

Glesne, C., & Peshkin, A. (1992). *Becoming qualitative researchers*. White Plains, NY: Longman.

References

Gottlieb, D., & Dede, C. (1983). *The social role of the personal computer.* Houston, TX: Hogg Foundation.

Greenfield, P. M. (1984). *Mind and media: The effects of television, video games, and computers.* Cambridge, MA: Harvard University Press.

Greenfield, P. M. (1985, Fall). Multimedia education: Why print isn't always best. *American Educator,* pp. 18–21, 36, 38.

Gripshover, N. A. (1984). The consequences of home computers for gender-role socialization: Defining a theoretical perspective. Paper presented at the Eastern Communication Association Conference, Philadelphia, PA.

Gross, N., Giacquinta, J. B., & Bernstein, M. (1971). *Implementing organizational innovations: A sociological analysis of planned educational change.* New York: Basic Books.

Gross, N., Mason, W. S., & McEachern, A. W. (1958). *Explorations in role analysis.* New York: Wiley.

Harel, I. (1991). *Children designers: Interdisciplinary constructions for learning and knowing mathematics in a computer-rich school.* Norwood, NJ: Ablex.

Hawkins, J. (1987). Computers and girls: Rethinking the issues. In R. Pea & K. Sheingold (Eds.), *Mirrors of minds: Patterns of experience in educational computing* (pp. 242–57). Norwood, NJ: Ablex.

Henderson, A. T. (1988). Parents are a school's best friend. *Phi Delta Kappan, 70,* 148–53.

Hess, R. D., & Miura, I. T. (1985). Gender differences in computer camps and classes. *Sex Roles, 13*(3–4), 193–203.

Hess, R. D., & McGarvey, L. J. (1987). School-relevant effects of educational uses of microcomputers in kindergarten classrooms and homes. *Journal of Educational Computing Research, 3,* 269–87.

Hill, R. H. (1985). Computers, people, and the home. In M. B. Sussman (Ed.), *Personal computers and the family* (pp. 27–40). New York: Haworth Press.

Hoban, P. (1985, April 29). Safe at home. *New York,* pp. 16–20.

Honebein, P. C., Chen, P., & Brescia, W. (1992). Applying cognitive apprenticeship to the design of a hypermedia learning environment. Paper presented at the annual meeting of the Association for Educational Communications and Technology, Washington, DC.

Howe, S. F. (1985, January). Interactive video: Salt and pepper technology. *Media and Methods,* pp. 8, 10–12.

References

Huberman, A. M., & Miles, M. B. (1984). *Innovation up close: How school improvement works*. New York: Plenum.

Hunt, R. A. (1985). Computers and families – an overview. In M. B. Sussman (Ed.), *Personal computers and the family* (pp. 11–25). New York: Haworth.

In the Holy Land. (1989, September). *Classroom Computer Learning*, p. 59.

Jennings, L. (1990, April 4). Studies link parental involvement, higher student achievement. *Education Week*, pp. 20–1.

Kanter, R. M. (1983). *The change masters*. New York: Simon & Schuster.

Katz, E. (1988). Personal computers: Where to put them so children will use them. Paper presented at the annual meeting of the American Educational Research Association, New Orleans, LA.

Katz, E. H. (1992). *Receptivity of home economics teachers in New York State to the home and career skills curriculum* (Doctoral Dissertation, New York University, 1992).

Kay, A. C. (1991, September). Computers, networks and education. *Scientific American*, pp. 138–43, 146, 148.

Kazlow, C. (1974). *Resistance to innovation in complex organizations: A test of two modes of resistance in a higher education setting* (Doctoral Dissertation, New York University, 1974).

Kazlow, C. (1977). Faculty receptivity to organizational change: A test of two explanations of resistance to innovations in higher education. *Journal of Research and Development in Higher Education*, *10*(2), 87–99.

Kepner, H. S., Jr. (1986). Issues regarding computers in the schools. In H. S. Kepner, Jr. (Ed.), *Computers in the classroom* (pp. 40–50). Washington, DC: NEA Professional Library.

Kinzer, C. K., Sherwood, R. D., Bauch, J. P., Saks, D. H., Clouse, R. W., & Deck, L. L. (1985). A compilation of ideas: Reactions to and comments on issues presented at the planning the school of the future conference. *Peabody Journal of Education*, *62*(2), 118–30.

Knapp, L. R. (1987, March). Teleconferencing: A new way of communicating for teachers and kids. *Classroom Computer Learning*, pp. 37–41.

Komoski, P. K. (1984, December). Educational computing: The burden of insuring quality. *Phi Delta Kappan*, *66*, 244–8.

Kozma, R. B. (1991). Learning with media. *Review of Educational Research*, *61*, 179–211.

Kreinberg, N., & Stage, E. K. (1983). EQUALS in computer technology. In J. Zimmerman (Ed.), *The technological woman: Interfacing with tomorrow*. New York: Praeger.

References

LaFrenz, D., & Friedman, J. E. (1989). Computers don't change education, teachers do! *Harvard Educational Review, 59*, 222–5.

Lane, P. A. (1993). *The receptivity of mediators to professional practice innovations: A test of status-related risk theory* (Doctoral Dissertation, New York University, 1993).

Lehrer, A. (1989, September). The '88 vote: Campaign for the White House. *Classroom Computer Learning*, pp. 18–19.

Lev, M. (1990, April 29). As the craze cools: A youth-based industry matures. *New York Times*, p. 10F.

Levin, H., & Meister, G. (1985). *Educational technology and computers: Promises, promises, always promises* (Project Report No. 85-A13). Stanford, CA: Institute for Research on Educational Finance and Governance.

Levin, J. E. (1990). *You can't just plug it in: Integrating the computer into the curriculum* (Doctoral Dissertation, New York University, 1990).

Lewis, P. H. (1988, August 7). The computer revolution revised. *New York Times*, pp. 15–17. (Sect. 4a).

Lewis, P. H. (1989, August 6). Child's play. *New York Times*, pp. 52, 54–5. (Sect. 4a).

Lewis, P. H. (1992, May 26). Summer and the computin's easy. *New York Times*, p. C7.

Lipman-Blumen, J. (1984). *Gender roles and power.* Englewood Cliffs, NJ: Prentice-Hall.

Lockheed, M. E. (1985). Women, girls, and computers: A first look at the evidence. *Sex Roles, 13*(3–4), 115–22.

Loucks-Horsley, S., & Hergert, I. (1985). *An action guide to school improvement.* Alexandria, VA: Association for Supervision and Curriculum Development.

McClain, L. (1983, April). A friendly introduction to videodisks. *Popular Computing*, pp. 79–83, 86.

McGill, D. C. (1989, June 5). Now, video game players can take show on the road. *New York Times*, pp. D1, D6.

McKibbin, W. L. (1986, April). Do drills make drones? *Incider*, pp. 52–5.

McKnight, G. B. (1986). *The computer in the family: Six case studies* (Doctoral Dissertation, Teachers College, 1986).

McLaughlin, M. W. (1987, Summer). Learning from experience: Lessons from policy implementation. *Educational Evaluation and Policy Analysis, 9*, 171–8.

References

McMahon, T. A., Carr, A. A., & Fishman, B. J. (1992). Hypermedia and constructionism: Three approaches. Paper presented at the annual meeting of the Association for Educational Communications and Technology, Washington, DC.

Mageau, T. (1992, January). Integrating an ILS: Two teaching models that work. *Electronic Learning*, pp. 17–22.

Making the grade. (1983). Task Force on Elementary and Secondary Education Policy. New York: Twentieth Century Fund.

Malone, T. W. (1984). What makes computer games fun? Guidelines for designing educational computer programs. In D. Peterson (Ed.), *Intelligent Schoolhouse* (pp. 78–92). Reston, VA: Reston.

Margalit, M. (1990). *Effective technology integration for disabled children: The family perspective.* New York: Springer-Verlag.

Marriott, M. (1991, March 20). Videodisks are integrated with computers for a versatile teaching tool. *New York Times*, p. B8.

Mehan, H. (1989, March). Microcomputers in classrooms: Educational technology or social practice? *Anthropology and Education Quarterly, 20*(1), 3–22.

Miles, M. B., & Huberman, A. M. (1984). *Qualitative data analysis.* Beverly Hills: Sage.

Miura, I. T. (1984). Processes contributing to individual differences in computer literacy. *Dissertation Abstracts International, 45*, 1934–5. (University Microfilms No. DA 8420593).

Mort, P. (1953). Educational adaptability. *School Executive, 73*, 1–23.

Multimedia: How it changes the way we teach and learn. (1991, September). *Electronic Learning*, pp. 22–6.

Multimedia takes personal computing by storm. (1992, January). *Electronic Learning*, p. 8.

Naisbitt, J. (1982). *Megatrends: Ten new directions transforming our lives.* New York: Warner.

A nation prepared: Teachers for the 21st century. (1986). [The Report of the Task Force on Teaching as a Profession]. Carnegie Forum on Education and the Economy. Princeton, NJ: Carnegie Foundation for the Advancement of Teaching.

A new compact for learning: Improving public elementary, middle, and secondary education results in the 1990s. (1991). The University of the State of New York: State Department of Education.

Nickerson, R. S. (1991, March). A minimalist approach to the paradox of sense making. *Educational Researcher, 20*(9), 24–6.

November, A. (1992, April). Digressions: Familyware. *Electronic Learning*, p. 50.

References

OERI. (1991, Fall). Parents as teachers. *Office of Educational Research and Instruction Bulletin,* pp. 4–6.

Oettinger, A. G. (1969). *Run, computer, run: The mythology of educational innovation.* (S. Marks, Collaborator). New York: Collier.

Office of Technology Assessment. (1988). *Power on: New tools for teaching and learning* [OTA-SET-379]. Washington, DC: U.S. Government Printing Office.

Olsen, R. (1988). *Preparing for a career in the 21st century.* Palo Alto: Computer Learning Month.

Olson, L. (1990, April 4). Parents as partners: Redefining the social contract between families and schools. *Education Week,* pp. 17–24.

Ortiz, C. (1992, January 20). Carmen Sandiego is leading children around the world. *New York Post,* p. 28.

Ost, D. H. (1991). The culture of teaching: Stability and change. In N. Wyner (Ed.), *Current perspectives on the culture of schools* (pp. 79–93). Cambridge, MA: Brookline.

Papert, S. (1980). *Mindstorms.* New York: Basic Books.

Perelman, L. J. (1992). School's out: Hyperlearning, the new technology, and the end of education. New York: William Morrow.

Perkins, D. N. (1983). Educational heaven: Promises and perils of instruction by video games. In S. S. Baughman & P. D. Clagett (Eds.), *Video games and human development* (pp. 33–40). Cambridge, MA: Monroe C. Gutman Library, Harvard Graduate School of Education.

Perkins, D. N. (1985). The fingertip effect: How information-processing technology shapes thinking. *Educational Researcher, 14*(7), 11–17.

Phi Delta Kappan. (1991). [Special Section]. *Phi Delta Kappan, 72,* 344–88.

Platt, J. (1992, Spring). "Case Study" in American methodological thought. *Current Sociology, 40*(1), 17–48.

Plummer, M., & Bowman, S. (Eds.). (1988). *Family activities guide.* Palo Alto: Computer Learning Month.

Polin, L. (1991). Vygotsky at the computer: A Soviet view of "tools" for learning. *The Computing Teacher, 19*(1), 25–7.

Polley, P., & Wenn, R. D. (1988). *Everything you need to know (but were afraid to ask kids) about computer learning.* Palo Alto: Computer Learning Month.

Pournelle, J. (1986, September 15). Schools fail to educate: Micros fill in the gap. *Infoworld,* p. 23.

References

Pournelle, J. (1989, November 6). Educational crisis is very real: Maybe computers can help. *Infoworld*, p. 23.

Powell, B. (1984, April). School computing programs: Still a long way from utopia. *Family Computing*, pp. 18, 20, 24.

Prescription Learning. (n.d.). *Take-home computer program* [Pamphlet]. Phoenix, AZ: Jostens Learning Corporation.

Ragsdale, R. G. (1988). *Permissible computing in education.* Westport, CT: Praeger.

Ramos, L. (1980). *Receptivity of Puerto Rican school teachers to four proposed innovations: An examination of status risk theory* (Doctoral Dissertation, New York University, 1980).

Redding, S. (1992, April). Parent scale to measure the efficacy of strategies to enhance the curriculum of the home. Paper presented at the annual meeting of the American Educational Research Association, San Francisco.

Reinhold, F. (1987, November/December). Online information services: You've come a long way, baby. *Electronic Learning*, pp. 36–8.

Resnick, L. B., & Johnson, A. (1988). Intelligent machines for intelligent people: Cognitive theory and the future of computer-assisted learning. In R. S. Nickerson & P. P. Zodhiates (Eds.), *Technology in education: Looking toward 2020* (pp. 139–68). Hillsdale, NJ: Erlbaum.

Responses to "Visions for the use of computers in classroom instruction." (1989). *Harvard Educational Review, 59*, 206–25.

Rich, D. (1988). *MegaSkills: How families can help children succeed in school and beyond.* Boston: Houghton Mifflin.

Roblyer, M., Castine, W., & King, F. (1988). *The effectiveness of computer applications for instruction: A review and synthesis of recent research findings.* New York: Haworth.

Rogers, E. M. (1962). *Diffusion of innovations.* New York: Free Press.

Rogers, E. M. (1983). *Diffusion of innovations* (3rd ed.). New York: Free Press.

Rogers, E. M. (1988). The intellectual foundation and history of the agricultural extension model. *Knowledge: Creation, Diffusion, Utilization, 9*, 492–510.

Rogers, E. M., & Larsen, J. K. (1984). *Silicon Valley fever.* New York: Basic Books.

Rosen, M. (1987, October). But wait, there's more. *Classroom Computer Learning*, pp. 50–5.

References

Ross, S. N., Smith, L. J., Morrison, G. R., & O'Dell, J. (1990). *What happens after ACOT: Outcomes for program graduates one year later* (ACOT Report No. 6). Cupertino, CA: Apple Classrooms of Tomorrow, Advanced Technology Group, Apple Computer, Inc.

Rothstein, E. (1990, April 26). Adventures in Never-Never Land. *New York Times*, pp. C1, C12.

Salomon, G. (1986). Computers in education: Setting a research agenda. In T. R. Cannings & S. W. Brown (Eds.), *The information age classroom: Using the computer as a tool* (pp. 12–16). Irvine, CA: Franklin, Beadle and Associates.

Salomon, G., & Gardner, H. (1986). The computer as educator: Lessons from television research. *Educational Researcher, 15*(1), 13–19.

Salpeter, J. (1986, November/December). Notes on the LOGO '86 Conference: Whatever happened to the Logo revolution? *Classroom Computer Learning*, pp. 48–9.

Salpeter, J. (1991, February). Beyond videodisks: Compact disks in the multimedia classroom. *Technology and Learning*, pp. 32–6, 38–40, 66–7.

Sanders, J., & Stone, A. (1986). *The neuter computer: Computers for girls and boys.* New York: Neal-Schuman.

Sarason, S. B. (1990). *The predictable failure of educational reform.* San Francisco: Jossey-Bass.

Schulz, E. (1991, January). Teaching with technology: But does it work? *Teacher Magazine*, p. 50.

Scott, T., Cole, M., & Engel, M. (1992). Computers and education: A cultural constructivist perspective. In G. Grant (Ed.), *Review of Research in Education, 5* (pp. 191–251). Washington, DC: American Educational Research Association.

Shalvoy, M. L. (1987a, January). Sunburst's Marge Kosel: Striving to set the software standard. *Electronic Learning*, pp. 24–5.

Shalvoy, M. L. (1987b, May/June). Core of Apple project is seeding home–school connection. *Electronic Learning*, p. 19.

Shao, M. (1989, July 17). Computers in school: A loser? or a lost opportunity? *Business Week*, pp. 108–9, 112.

Sheingold, K., Hawkins, J., & Char, C. (1984). *"I'm the thinkist, you're the typist": The interaction of technology and the social life of classrooms* (Technical Report No. 27). New York: Bank Street College.

Sheingold, K., Martin, L. M. V., & Endreweit, M. E. (1987). Preparing urban teachers for the technological future. In R. D. Pea & K. Sheingold (Eds.), *Mirrors of minds: Patterns of experience in educational computing* (pp. 67–85). Norwood, NJ: Ablex.

References

Silvern, S. B. (1987). Learning options with microcomputers: Now and in the future. In B. Hatcher (Ed.), *Learning opportunities beyond the school* (pp. 75–80). Wheaton, MD: Association for Childhood Education International.

Simonsen, R., & Hessel, B. (1985, November). Nation's computer owners. *Popular Computing,* pp. 67–72.

Sivin, J. P., & Bialo, E. R. (Comp. & Ed.). (1988, November/December). The OTA report: Educational software quantity, quality, and the marketplace. *Classroom Computer Learning,* pp. 54–7.

Sloan, D. (Ed.). (1985). *The computer in education: A critical perspective.* New York: Teachers College Press.

Snodgrass, D. (1991, Spring). The parent connection. *Adolescence, 26,* 83–7.

Snyder, T., & Palmer, J. (1986). *In search of the most amazing thing: Children, education, and computers.* Reading, MA: Addison-Wesley.

Solomon, G. (1989, May). Heard it, read it, and saw it on the grapevine. *Electronic Learning,* pp. 18–19.

Spicer, E. (1952). *Human problems in technological change.* New York: Russell Sage.

Stacey, J. (1991, August 5). More homes have PC's. *USA Today,* p. 1.

Strauss, A., & Corbin, J. (1990). *Basis of qualitative research.* Newbury Park, CA: Sage.

Summers, J. A., Bertsch, R., & Smith, L. (1989). Indiana's Buddy System Project puts Macintoshes in students' homes. *T.H.E. Journal,* pp. 41–4.

Sussman, M. B. (Ed.). (1985). *Personal computers and the family.* New York: Haworth Press.

Sutton, R. E. (1991). Equity and computers in the schools: A decade of research. *Review of Educational Research, 61,* 475–503.

Swap, S. M. (1991). Can parent involvement lead to increased student achievement in urban schools? Paper presented at the annual meeting of the American Educational Research Association, Chicago, IL.

Symposium: Visions for the use of computers in classroom instruction. (1989). *Harvard Educational Review, 59,* 50–86.

Taylor, P. (Ed.). (1985, May). RAC examines buyers of home computers. *The Sampler, 37,* 14.

Taylor, R. P. (Ed.). (1980). *The computer in the school: Tutor, tool, tutee.* New York: Teachers College Press.

References

Technology links classroom and home. (1991, June 10). *UFT Bulletin*, p. 6A.

Tinnell, C. S. (1985). An ethnographic look at personal computers in a family setting. In M. B. Sussman (Ed.), *Personal computers and the family* (pp. 59–69). New York: Haworth.

Tornatzky, L. G., Eveland, J. D., Boylan, M. G., Hetzner, W. A., Johnson, E. C., Roitman, D., & Schneider, J. (1983). *The process of technological innovation: Reviewing the literature.* Washington, DC: National Science Foundation.

Turkle, S. (1984). *The second self.* New York: Simon & Schuster.

Van Gelder, L. (1985, January). Help for technophobes: Think of your computer as just another appliance. *MS.*, pp. 89–91.

Vygotsky, L. S. (1978). *Mind in society: The development of higher psychological processes* (M. Cole, V. John-Steiner, S. Scribner, & E. Souberman, Eds.). Cambridge, MA: Harvard University Press.

Wakefield, R. (1983, October). Computers to revolutionize family–school relationship. *American Family, 6*(9), 1.

Wald, M. L. (1991, February 16). Buying a personal computer: The choices can be daunting. *New York Times*, p. 52.

Walde, A. C., & Baker, K. (1990). How teachers view the parents' role in education. *Phi Delta Kappan, 72*, 319–22.

Watkins, B., & Brimm, D. (1985). The adoption and use of microcomputers in homes and elementary schools. In M. Chen & W. Paisley (Eds.), *Children and microcomputers: Research on the newest medium* (pp. 129–50). Beverly Hills: Sage.

Weizenbaum, J. (1976). *Computer power and human reason: From judgment to calculation.* New York: W. H. Freeman.

West, P. (1992, February 5). Despite first impressions, experts hail software's quality gains. *Education Week*, pp. 12–13.

White, K. R., Taylor, M. J., & Moss, V. D. (1992, Spring). Does research support claims about the benefits of involving parents in early intervention programs? *Review of Educational Research, 62*, 92–125.

Williams, F., Coulombe, J. & Lievrouw, L. (1983). Children's attitudes toward small computers: A preliminary study. *Education Communication and Technology Journal, 31*(1), 3–7.

Williams, F., & Williams, V. (1985). *Success with educational software.* New York: Praeger.

Winn, T., & Coleman, I. (1989). Urban and rural: A dialogue about computers in schools. *Harvard Educational Review, 59*, 212–17.

Withrow, F. B. (1985, Fall). Videodisks: The thinking person's audiovisual. *American Educator*, pp. 22–5, 40, 42.

References

Wolins, I. (1988). The family as educator: Effects of parent–child interaction on microcomputer use. Paper presented at the annual meeting of the American Educational Research Association, New Orleans, LA.

Yarcheski, A., & Mahon, N. E. (1985). The unification model in nursing: A study of receptivity among nurse educators in the United States. *Nursing Research, 34*(2), 120–5.

Yarcheski, A., & Mahon, N. E. (1986). The unification model in nursing: Risk-receptivity profiles among deans, tenured and nontenured faculty in the United States. *Western Journal of Nursing Research, 8*(1), 63–81.

Zimmerman, J. (Ed.). (1983). *The technological woman: Interfacing with tomorrow.* New York: Praeger.

Zimmerman, J. (1987). *Once upon the future: A woman's guide to tomorrow's technology.* New York: Methuen.

Name Index

Subject Index